WHO WAS THAT LADY I SAW YOU WITH?

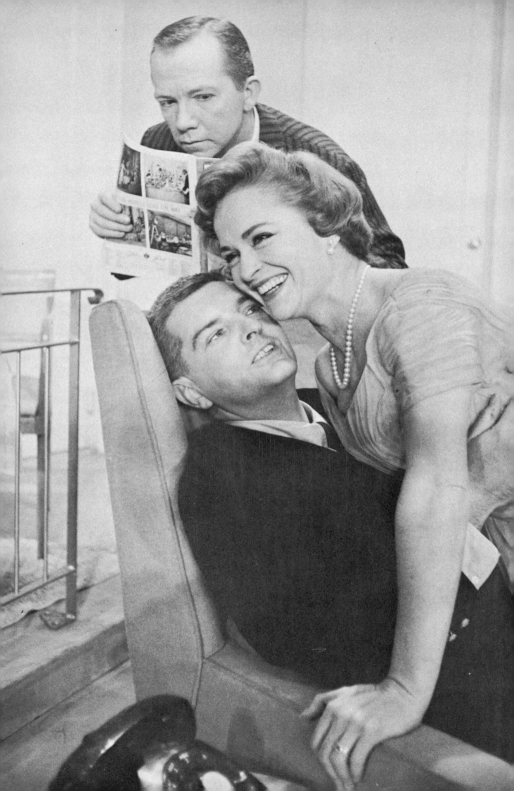

Who was that lady I saw you with?

A new comedy by NORMAN KRASNA

Random House, New York

Photographs by courtesy of Slim Aarons

Manufactured in the United States of America

For ERLE,
who made me do it

WHO WAS THAT LADY I SAW YOU WITH? *was first presented by
Leland Hayward at the Martin Beck Theatre, New York City,
on March 3, 1958, with the following cast:*

(IN ORDER OF APPEARANCE)

DAVID WILLIAMS	Peter Lind Hayes
MICHAEL HANEY	Ray Walston
SCHULTZ	Wallace Rooney
ANN WILLIAMS	Mary Healy
ROBERT DOYLE	William Swetland
SECRETARY	Joan Morgan
HARRY POWELL	Roland Winters
WAITER	Stephen C. Cheng
LEE WONG	Richard Kuen Loo
GLORIA COOGLE	Roxanne Arlen
FLORENCE COOGLE	Virginia de Luce
JOE BENDIX	Pete Gumeny
EVANS	Robert Burr
PARKER	Frank Milan
ORLOV	Larry Storch
BELKA	Gregory Morton
FIRST TENANT	Pete Gumeny
SECOND TENANT	Pamela Curran
BUILDING EMPLOYEE	W. Edgar Rooney
THIRD TENANT	Joan Morgan
MCCARTHY	Dan Frazer

Directed by Alex Segal

Settings by Rouben Ter-Arutunian

Costumes by Ruth Morley

Music by Bernard Green

Synopsis of Scenes

ACT ONE

Act Two

(Printed on the Curtain)

The following characters and events depicted in this play are fictitious. Any similarity to actual persons, living or dead, is purely coincidental.

The Producer

United Airlines
Groucho Marx
Columbia University
The Federal Bureau of Investigation
Reno
Signal Corps, United States Army
Psi Epsilon
The Cathedral of Notre Dame
Scotland Yard
William C. Paley
Lee Wong's Restaurant
Jack Benny
CBS
Sing Sing
Golden Dairy Milk
The Boy Scouts of America
Arlington Cemetery
Madame Chiang Kai-shek
Tums
Lucky Strike
The Empire State Building
and
J. EDGAR HOOVER

WHO WAS THAT LADY I SAW YOU WITH?

ACT ONE

ACT ONE

Scene One

A small office befitting an assistant professor of advanced chemistry at Columbia University. Files, charts, a couch, and a table holding flasks and a Bunsen burner are apparent.

DAVID WILLIAMS *is on stage. He is twenty-seven, wears a smock, and when his face is in repose most likable. At the moment, however, it is in a still grimace of weeping, and tears have made two visible, glistening paths down his cheeks. He looks at the beaker in his hand. The beaker is half filled and colorless. He brings it to his mouth, clearly on a crying jag.*

The door opens, admitting MICHAEL HANEY. MIKE *and* DAVID *graduated from college together, shop at Brooks Brothers, and usually react alike to most situations, but five years of marriage for one has differed their metabolisms.* MICHAEL *wears a topcoat and carries a porkpie hat.*

MIKE (*From the door*) I came as fast as I could! (DAVID *looks to him, his expression one of great unhappiness, but he does not speak*) What's the matter? (DAVID *is still unable to speak, merely looking at* MIKE) What's the matter?

DAVID Ann's left me. (MIKE *frowns, and sits, waiting for more, not taking his eyes from* DAVID) She's going to get a divorce.

3

(A moment's solemnity, and DAVID *lifts the beaker to his lips, but* MIKE *reaches for it and takes it out of his hand. He sniffs it)*

MIKE   Is this what chemistry professors drink? What is it?

DAVID *(Wan voice)*   Alcohol, benzaldehyde and dextrose.
(MIKE *puts the beaker down, away from* DAVID)

MIKE   You got any more classes today? (DAVID *shakes his head*)
What happened?

DAVID   Ann walked in here unexpectedly and caught me.

MIKE   Caught you with whom?

DAVID   With a student.
(MIKE *grimaces knowingly and looks around, settling on the couch, re-creating the scene*)

MIKE   Oh! What were you doing?

DAVID   I was kissing a girl.

MIKE   Kissing? That all you were doing?

DAVID   That's all.

MIKE   What kind of kissing? On the couch, all tangled up?

DAVID *(Reluctant to bare all)*   We were standing up. In the middle of the room.

MIKE   Dressed? Both of you? Either of you?

4

DAVID Certainly we were dressed! What's the matter with you? Are you crazy?

MIKE You kiss a girl without locking the door and you call me crazy?

DAVID I didn't know this girl was going to kiss me.

MIKE Oh, *she* kissed *you?* She jumped you, from behind?

DAVID She kissed me first.

MIKE And when Ann came in you were pushing her away?

DAVID When someone kisses you you just can't stand there.

MIKE No, you can't. Common courtesy.

DAVID (*Strong*) She's divorcing me, Mike! Our life together is over!

MIKE Now, now, don't get panicky. A woman saying she'll get a divorce and a woman getting a divorce are two different things.

DAVID Ann's not like other women! She's insanely jealous! You don't know her!

MIKE She's like other women. She'll yell bloody murder but it'll all come down to your ponying up an imitation pearl necklace or whatever you can't afford, and a second honeymoon trip to someplace you don't want to go, and that'll be the end of it.

DAVID   I often wondered why you were still single. It's clear to me now.

MIKE   (*Getting up*)   It ought to be. I don't care for jams like this. (*He looks at the beaker, puts his finger in it, and tastes it. He lifts the beaker to his mouth and sips*) Not bad. Kind of scotchy, with a vodka undertone. Why don't you market it? Call it "Scotchka." Well, I've got a lot of work to do—

DAVID   Aren't you going to help me?

MIKE   Help you how?

DAVID   I don't know how! That's why I called you!

MIKE   My boy, if I could invent an excuse that would satisfy a wife catching a husband I wouldn't be writing TV programs. I'd rent out my excuse on a royalty basis, so much per use per husband, and live on the income. (*A wave of the hat*) See you around.

DAVID   (*Unbelieving*)   You're leaving? You're not even going to *try* to help?

MIKE   (*Shakes his head*)   Millions of husbands have tried to lick this. The pearl necklace and the second honeymoon, that's the only solution. Take my word for it. Don't try to save money.

DAVID   Bribery won't work with Ann! I tell you she'll divorce me!

MIKE   (*At the door*)   Not for kissing a student.
    (*The phone rings.* DAVID *looks toward it*)

6

MIKE Well, answer it. It's your wife. And it's going to be, "Don't come home, I won't let you in," but you'll notice she won't change the lock on the door!

DAVID *(Taking the phone)* Hello . . . Yes, this is Mr. Williams . . .

MIKE Well?

DAVID It's United Airlines. . . . They're confirming Mrs. Williams' space to Reno, Nevada. For nine o'clock tonight. Thank you.
     (He hangs up, forlorn)

MIKE *(Impressed)* Reno? *(He whistles)* Hey!

DAVID *(Far away)* Now do you believe me?

MIKE *(Sitting)* That's outside the rules.

DAVID Ann doesn't go by the rules. You don't know her like I do.

MIKE *(Thinking)* Of course that Reno move could be a gesture. Women'll do that.

DAVID It's no gesture! She means it! She's got a jealousy phobia! She'll go through with it. *(He can't control himself. Sobs)* Mike, I can't lose her! I love her!

MIKE *(Finally touched)* Yeah, I guess you do at that. I'm not a marriage booster myself but you two kind of match. It'd be a shame if you busted up.

7

DAVID   Then help me! Can't you invent some reason why I was kissing that girl?

MIKE   Listen, you can't invent yourself out of everything.

DAVID   You can! I've seen you invent stories in front of my eyes. Sometimes we're eating dinner and between the shrimp cocktail and the soup you've got the whole thing planned out.

MIKE   It's not the same.

DAVID   Why isn't it?

MIKE   Well, a writer thinks of a solution first, how to get *out* of a jam. Then, after he has that, he puts the hero *into* that jam. But it's a special jam he knows how to get out of. You've started with a whole foolproof jam already. I'm kind of limited.

DAVID   Don't take a defeatist attitude, Mike. You can do it. I'm sure you can. Pretend I'm a character in a story you're writing. My wife thinks I'm cheating. Show her she's wrong, she's mistaken in what she saw!

MIKE   Groucho used to have a line like that. "Who are you going to believe, me or your own eyes?"

DAVID   Mike! No jokes! Not now! (*Pointing to the phone*) She's got a reservation to Reno! Think of something!

MIKE   (*Still reluctant*)   I've got a lot of work piled up—

DAVID   (*A wail*)   Mike!

8

MIKE (*Wavering*) Well . . .
  (DAVID *snatches the beaker and gives it to him.* MIKE *looks at it and takes a drink*)

DAVID (*Grateful*) I'll never forget you for this, Mike.

MIKE Wait a minute, you're not out of the woods yet.
  (MIKE *takes his coat off, and sits, stretched out, his feet propped up, while* DAVID *prepares a batch of "Scotchka" from different flasks and containers*)

DAVID Yes I am! Once you've decided to help me I'm all right! You're a genius! Oh, I admit I've belittled your programs in the past. You know why? I've analyzed myself. Deep down I'm jealous. Those programs of yours are wonderful. They're clever, and touching, and true to life. And point a moral besides!

MIKE I try to make them that. It's interesting you noticed about the moral. We get thousands of letters from ministers, from people in jail, from dope addicts, a real cross section of American life, and—

DAVID (*Interrupting, anxious to get* MIKE *back on the problem at hand*) We haven't got much time, Mike—

MIKE (*A struggle to leave the subject*) Yeah. Okay, fill me in. What exactly did Ann do when she caught you?

DAVID (*Only occasionally halting his preparation while he talks*) Well, when she opened that door and saw me kissing this girl she jumped back and ran down the hall. I ran after her but she was already in the elevator, so I ran down the stairs.

9

I fell down a whole flight—(*He cuts this diversion short*) I caught her on the street but she wouldn't talk to me. Students started collecting and she jumped in a cab. All she said through the window of the cab was, "You pack up and be out of that apartment by seven o'clock!"

MIKE   Seven o'clock. That's three hours. That's not very much time.

DAVID   We can do it, Mike! I'm sure we can! (*A correction*) *You* can!

MIKE   What have we got to go on? (*Staring at* DAVID, *thinking out loud*) *Who* are our characters? What do they do for a living?

DAVID   I'm an assistant chemistry professor at Columbia University, making sixty-five hundred dollars a year. Does it help if I talk like that? (MIKE *is deep in thought;* DAVID *takes that for assent*) I'm also in charge of student admissions.

MIKE   (*Far away*)   In charge of admissions.

DAVID   That girl who kissed me wanted to be transferred from a morning class to an afternoon class. She's a foreign exchange student. Well, I did it and she was grateful . . . and . . . (MIKE *puts his head back, grimacing*)

MIKE   (*Mumbling*)   A foreign exchange student . . . (DAVID *has poured out two beakers; now gives* MIKE *one.* MIKE *takes them both*)

DAVID   Hey, that's mine. That's ninety proof. Are you going to be able to think?

10

MIKE   I can think lying down! We don't know yet what you're
going to have to do. (*He takes a gulp while* DAVID *watches.
He leans back again*) Ann's character. What is she?

DAVID   She's my wife.

MIKE   Housewife. Overemotional. Overimpulsive.

DAVID   That's what she is! You've hit it on the head! Everything's extreme with her! If she gets an idea in her head . . .
        (*He trails off, not wanting to disturb* MIKE's *evident
        concentration*)

MIKE   (*Mumbling to the ceiling—unintelligible.* DAVID *sits on the
edge of the chair, watching him hopefully*)   Aaah . . . mm-
mmm . . . aaaaah.

DAVID   Would you like some music? I could put the radio on.
(*No answer, but more mumbling.* MIKE *seems to have something. He cocks his head.* DAVID *leans forward.* MIKE *decides
against his notion.* DAVID *relaxes.* MIKE *looks around, sees the
newspaper beside him. He takes it, putting his drink down.
He unfolds it, and settles into reading*) Are you going to read
a newspaper? (*No answer*) We haven't got much time. (*No
answer.* MIKE *is scanning the headlines of the stories. He
opens the paper*) Mike, for God's sake, are you going to
help me, or aren't you? This is no time for relaxing— (MIKE
*has discovered something in the paper, and now looks far off,
lost in thought. His expression is one of grim concentration*)
What's the matter? (MIKE *nods*) Have you got something,
Mike? (MIKE *is still far off, creating. He nods again to himself*) Have you, Mike? (*Still nothing*) Talk to me!

MIKE *(Finally focusing on him)* Yes, I've got something.

DAVID What is it?

MIKE It'll need a lot of acting on your part. Sincere acting.

DAVID I'll be sincere. And it won't be acting.

MIKE *(Smiling)* You ready?

DAVID *(Smiling back)* Shoot.

MIKE The reason you were kissing that girl is because— *(He chuckles, so does* DAVID, *nodding in anticipation)* You're working for the F.B.I.

DAVID *(It hasn't sunk in)* What's that?

MIKE You're doing special work for the F.B.I. That's why you were kissing her!

DAVID WHAT? The F.B.I.? Me!

MIKE You haven't heard it all yet!

DAVID I don't want to hear another word, you moron! That's your idea of helping me! Making me an F.B.I. man! And you think Ann'd believe that? What do you think she is, one of the idiots watching your stupid program? She'd spit in my eye if I told her a story like that! Not only that, she'd say she was *ashamed* of me! Oh, go away! Let me alone!

MIKE I'm puzzled why I don't leave. I think it's because you're so childlike that taking offense doesn't become me.

DAVID All right, I'm childlike, and making me an F.B.I. man is brilliant, and stop helping me.

MIKE (*Calm—quietly*) I didn't just make up that story. I'm going to tell you something now. And if you ever repeat it, if you ever divulge it to a living soul, I swear, by everything I hold sacred, I'll kill you. (*This tone is in such contrast to his normal attitude that* DAVID's *attention is arrested.* MIKE *reaches down and takes off his shoe. He pulls off his sock and holds his foot up*) What do you see?

DAVID What is that?

MIKE (*Rattling it off*) My number is five seven nine seven three. My F.B.I. name is Harold Evans. I'm in Section Six of the Twelfth New York Division. My superior is known to me by the name of Carl Edmundson. My contact is Post Office Box number six twenty-seven in the post office at Wall and Broad. The telephone number is Hanover two—nine one, seven one. I've been an F.B.I. supplementary agent for seven years, and I've never spent an evening with you that I haven't checked in by phone between eleven and twelve o'clock, if you'll remember back. How do you like them apples, you silly bastard?

DAVID (*Overwhelmed*) When did you join the F.B.I.? We lived together. I always knew where you were.

MIKE You did, eh? When we were in the army and I was transferred to the Signal Corps at Fort Monmouth didn't it ever seem peculiar to you that after I was trained for six months they sent me *back* to the unit? I never even saw Fort

Monmouth! I was at the F.B.I. academy in Quantico, Virginia! Even the letters I sent you were rerouted to have a Fort Monmouth postmark! You don't mind if the government doesn't want us to tell our friends, do you?

DAVID Boy, that's a surprise!

MIKE I'll give you another little surprise! You know that tall girl with the Italian haircut you and Ann thought kind of light-headed? She's an F.B.I. agent! How's that for an eye opener?

DAVID (*Shaking his head*) Wow!

MIKE What's so "wow" about it? You read every day in the papers about undercover F.B.I. men. Where do you think we come from? Do you think the stork brings us?

DAVID What do you do? Do you spy on people?

MIKE What else would you like to know, big nose?

DAVID I'm sorry.

MIKE I'm violating my oath, which I didn't think I'd ever do, no matter what the provocation.

DAVID (*Moved*) I'm very grateful.

MIKE We've got a lot of details to provide for you in the next three hours! I don't know if we can even make it! And sitting here arguing with you isn't helping any! Take your shoe off! (*He takes a pen from his pocket*) Come on! (DAVID *does, quickly.* MIKE *jabs him with the pen*) It's supposed to be tattooed on!

DAVID Ow! Has every F.B.I. man got three green dots on his heel?

MIKE (*No change of tone*) I don't know about the F.B.I., but everyone in the Cornell chapter of Psi Epsilon fraternity has!

DAVID (*It's slowly sinking in*) Psi Epsilon fraternity? What are you talking about?

MIKE Hold your foot still!

DAVID Say, are you in the F.B.I., or aren't you?

MIKE Me? In the F.B.I.? Why, I couldn't even get to be an Eagle Scout, you jackass! What's the matter with you?
(*He jabs him again*)

DAVID (*Trying to get his leg back, but unable to*) Ow! Then what the hell are you doing?

MIKE I'm saving your marriage, you dumb bunny! I convinced you I was in the F.B.I., didn't I? Well, we can certainly convince your stupid wife!
(*Another jab*)

DAVID (*Dazed, but defensive*) Ow! She's not stupid!

MIKE She's stupid enough! And if you invent enough details you can convince anybody! Especially if *I* invent 'em!
(*He jabs*)

DAVID Ow! Ow! That's *four* dots! You said three!

MIKE (*Surveying his handiwork*) I just promoted you. J. Edgar Hoover's got seven! Fine man, J. Edgar Hoover. Pleasure to work for him. (*He goes to the phone and dials*) Hello, CBS? Give me Schultz in the property department! (*He puts the phone down, goes to* DAVID *and shakes his foot*) Let it dry! Wave your foot around!

(MIKE *goes back to the phone*)

Scene Two

The lights come up in inset, upper right, showing SCHULTZ *in the Columbia Broadcasting shop.*

SCHULTZ (*Into phone*) Schultz speaking.

MIKE (*Into phone*) Schultzie! This is Mike Haney. I need a couple of props for my program. First, an F.B.I. revolver—

SCHULTZ (*Writing this down*) F.B.I. revolver—

MIKE Second, I want an F.B.I. identification card. It's got to look real, we're using it in close-up. With the actor's picture on it. I'll bring the actor over in ten minutes.

SCHULTZ All right.

MIKE What time will it be ready?

SCHULTZ Tomorrow. Three o'clock.

MIKE Tomorrow? Are you kidding? That F.B.I. card's being used tonight!

SCHULTZ Tonight? It's impossible.

MIKE Why is it impossible? You've always made cards before while I waited!

SCHULTZ Sure, plain, printed cards! But an F.B.I. card! The picture has to go to the photoengraver! And also the finger-prints! Then the whole thing goes in a plastic mold and is baked in plastic. It takes time! The oven isn't even heated! I'm not a magician!

MIKE Schultz, the performance starts at seven o'clock sharp! If the program doesn't go on, you'll take the rap! You know what they're like upstairs! (SCHULTZ *stares in horror.* MIKE *listens for a moment, then, with a satisfied smile, puts the receiver down and begins to hurry* DAVID *out the door*) We've got to get over to CBS!
(*They exit*)

SCHULTZ (*Dials frantically*) Sam! Start the plastic oven! . . . I don't care what time it is! . . . Complain to Mr. Paley! . . . Sam, don't give me a hard time, I'm also in the union! . . . We're in show business, Sam! You can't be in show business and eat on time, too!

The lights black out

SCENE THREE

The interior of the WILLIAMS' *living room. The decor befits an assistant professor.*
At curtain rise the stage is dark. Two cigarettes are glowing. Seated, DAVID *and* MIKE *are vaguely seen behind the cigarettes.*

DAVID   What time is it?

MIKE   You just asked me.

DAVID   Well, I'm asking you again.

MIKE   Seven fifteen.

DAVID   She's fifteen minutes late.

MIKE   She wants to be sure you're out of the apartment.

DAVID   Maybe you're fast.

MIKE   I'm not fast.

DAVID   I'm going to turn the light on and look at my watch.

MIKE   If she sees a light under the door she won't come in.
   (DAVID *turns on the light*)

DAVID   She couldn't be out in the hall without us knowing it, we'd've heard the elevator door open.

MIKE   She may be across the street seeing if the window is light.

DAVID (*He looks toward it*)   Yeah. (*He hurriedly turns off the light, leaving the room dark again. He puffs violently on the cigarette. We see the glow and also his wrist near his face*) It's seven sixteen.

MIKE   You might more profitably employ this time going over your scene.

DAVID   You've only told me what to say, how do we know what she'll answer?

MIKE   What's said isn't as important as how it's said. Be indignant! Attack, and keep attacking! In a loud voice!

DAVID (*Doubtfully*)   Mike, do you think she'll believe that story?

MIKE   She'll have to prove it's a lie! And we've got the details covered!

DAVID   How can we be sure she won't pick a detail we haven't got covered?

MIKE   We can't be sure! That's where we have to be clever! Force her into one of our details! After she sees your green dots she may ask to see mine! I'll refuse! Whether you're an F.B.I. man or not'll get obscured by the argument over whether I've *got* green dots or not! That's the kind of break we have to look for!

DAVID (*Doubtfully*)   I don't think it's going to work, Mike—

MIKE (*Annoyed*)   It may not!

DAVID   I'll be worse off than I was before.

MIKE   I thought you couldn't be worse off! Listen, it's no skin off my nose whether you try this or not! Give her the pearl necklace! The truth is you *are* running some risk if it doesn't come off, and I'm not even sure you can do it right! (DAVID *is undecided*) And if it'll help you make up your mind, I don't believe she'll divorce you! The safest thing you can do is throw yourself at her feet and start crying! I know you can do that well!

> (DAVID *begins to cry. We hear the elevator door open and close*)

DAVID   The elevator! Here she comes!

MIKE   Well? What about it?

DAVID (*A moan*)   Oh—

MIKE (*Louder*)   Well?

DAVID (*He nods, wetting his lips*)   I'm nervous!

MIKE   Well, stop it. Breathe in! (DAVID *does, one huge breath, which he holds*) Out, too, you idiot!

> (DAVID *exhales. He breathes in and out, audibly. The cigarettes are doused. We hear a key in the lock, the door opens, and* ANN *turns the light on, closing the door and entering without noticing the occupants. Both men are standing.* ANN *is beautiful; we love her immediately. Now she sees them. She stops, turns, and opens the door again, exciting, flicking off the light as she goes, and slamming the door behind her. Dark again.* DAVID *is heard crying. The door opens slowly.* ANN'S *hand is seen flicking on the light. Now she enters again, going to the closet, taking her suitcase, which she opens on the sofa, ignoring the men*)

DAVID (*Humbly*)   Don't leave, Ann. I only want a few minutes.

ANN   There's nothing to be gained by talk.

DAVID   A few minutes, Ann.

ANN   There'll only be bitterness, I thought we might be spared that.

DAVID   Give me five minutes. That's a minute for each year of our marriage. Is that too much?
(*She sits, keeping her coat on*)

ANN   Only five minutes.
(*She looks toward* MIKE, *who has seated himself, disinterestedly*)

DAVID   You know I love you, Ann. I've always loved you. I'll never love anyone else.

ANN   I'm not interested.

DAVID   And you love me. Your feelings are hurt, but you love me.

ANN   I don't love you at all. I've blotted you out of my memory.

DAVID   You could never blot me out of your memory.

ANN   That's typically vain of you.

DAVID   Have you blotted out the memory of our sabbatical in Paris? When we lost our money and lived off a case of sardines for a month, and could never eat them again?

ANN (*She doesn't look at him*)   Yes, I have.

DAVID Have you blotted out what we said to each other kneeling in Notre Dame?

ANN Yes.

DAVID (*With some heat*) Well, do you remember the day we fell in the lake and had to dry our clothes in the barn? The day we got engaged?
> (*She glares at him, and then at* MIKE, *who seems most interested in this last revelation*)

MIKE Don't mind me.

ANN If there was anything I needed to emphasize the gulf that exists between us, the wide, deep, cavernous gulf of two people a million light miles apart in morals and sensitivity, it would be this instance of attempting a reconciliation in front of a third person. And I use "person" in the figurative sense!

MIKE (*Calmly*) You don't like me?

ANN No, I never liked you. And I attempted to show you!

MIKE Oh, you got the message across.

ANN I believe you're largely responsible for his moral depravity. You're not a bachelor, you're a libertine! Bringing those shoddy girls into this house for dinner, a new one a week! Dangling your conquests in front of this impressionable adolescent! He was bound to imitate you, even if he had character, which he certainly has not!

MIKE (*To* DAVID) I can't stay all evening.

ANN Who's keeping you?

DAVID Ann!

23

ANN (*Standing up*)   I don't see that we're accomplishing any-thing! I'll thank you to do me the final courtesy of leaving! Now!
> (DAVID *looks at* MIKE, *and puts his hands out helplessly*)

DAVID   I'm going to have to tell her.

MIKE   You're over twenty-one. I urge you not to, but I can't stop you.
> (ANN *looks from one to the other, slightly thrown off guard*)

DAVID   I'm sorry, but I'm going to.

MIKE (*Sharp*)   You know the consequences!

DAVID   My God, you act as if I'm a traitor!

MIKE   No, you're not a traitor at all. Just the opposite. You've done more than your duty as a citizen. Of course the fact that you can do still more, that you've been trained and have an obligation to your country, maybe that's bothering your conscience.

DAVID (*Tortured*)   Yes, it is! (*To* ANN) I'm warning you! I'm not afraid of your not forgiving me for kissing that girl! I've got an excuse! But it'll be on your head if you make me tell you! You'll be sorry! This is your last chance! Are you going to forget about what you saw in the office or not!

ANN (*Bewildered, but not beaten*)   Certainly not!

DAVID   All right!
> (*He walks up to her and pushes her back in the chair*)

MIKE (*A warning*)   David! Your last chance!

DAVID   The hell with you! (*To* ANN) I was kissing that girl in the performance of my duty! I'm a member of the F.B.I.!

MIKE (*Loud*)   You're separated from the service!
(ANN *looks at him and stands up*)

ANN   I'm too much of a lady to spit in your eye, but I'll tell you this. I'm ashamed of you! I gave you credit for better than that!

DAVID (*Loud*)   I'm telling you the truth!

MIKE (*Louder*)   You're out!

ANN (*Scornfully*)   You in the F.B.I.! An assistant chemistry professor!

DAVID (*Louder*)   An assistant registrar in charge of admissions! Do *you* know what scientists work in the Columbia laboratories? On germ warfare? On radioactivity?

MIKE (*Loud*)   Shut up!

DAVID (*On and on*)   Have you an idea what some country would give just to know the *names* of these scientists, so they could tell what fields we're working in? And do you know who has all those names? Me! (*Pointing*) In my head! That's why the F.B.I. put me in that job! That's why I've stayed in that job! On orders!

MIKE   You've talked enough!

ANN (*Shaken, but not convinced*)   I don't believe you. When could you have joined the F.B.I.? I always knew where you were.

DAVID (*Attacking*) I joined them when I was in the army! I was trained while I was in the army! You read every day in the papers about undercover F.B.I. men! Where do you think we come from? The stork! (*High sarcasm*) And you don't mind if the government doesn't want us to tell our wives, do you? You big know it all, you think you're so smart! That tall girl he had here with the Italian haircut, the one you didn't think was so bright? *She's* an F.B.I. agent!—

MIKE (*A roar*) Shut your mouth!
(*He puts his hand over* DAVID's *mouth, and* DAVID *fights him off.* DAVID *sits down and tears off his shoe;* ANN *watches fascinated*)

DAVID I'll show you how much you know about me! (*Off comes his sock. He holds his heel up to her*) Here!

ANN What's that? I've never seen that before.

DAVID When did you ever look? You see four green dots? The girl with the Italian haircut's got five! J. Edgar Hoover's got seven!
(*He puts his sock back*)

MIKE I'll take your revolver, please.

DAVID I'm not going to give it to you!
(*He puts his shoe back*)

MIKE This is no time for you to act stupid. You've had your quota for the day. Give me your gun! And your identification card!

DAVID I'm not going to! (*He stands up*) I'm a good agent. I've never fallen down on anything! I've had compliments from Washington. I'm staying in the bureau.

26

MIKE   Give me your gun and your identification card, and right now!

DAVID   Mike, we've been through a lot together! What's changed that's made me useless to the bureau? Ann knows, but she won't tell! She'll take an oath that what she's heard here will never pass her lips! Won't you, dear? (*The men look toward her, hopeful for a hint of their success.* ANN *isn't sure of anything. Her mind is racing, she's puzzled. She sits*) We can trust her. She'd never go back on her word. Mike, I'm asking you as a friend. My closest friend. Please let me stay in the service!

MIKE   Don't ask me what I can't do. It's not up to me. I'll plead your case. That's all I can do.

DAVID   Thank you, Mike. That's all I ask. I'll never forget you. And neither will Ann. Will you, Ann?
   (*Still no move from the watching* ANN. *The men glance at her and at each other, aware that success or failure is in the balance*)

MIKE   I'll have to ask you for your gun and identification card until your case is decided.
   (DAVID *goes to the rear wall, stands on the chair, unscrews the lamp, and extracts the revolver. He hands it to* MIKE, *trying to sneak a look at the effect it's had upon* ANN)

DAVID (*Sadly*)   My gun.
   (*He takes a penknife from his pocket, opens it, goes to a picture on the wall, fishes between the frame and the picture, and comes out with a card. He takes it to* MIKE)

27

DAVID   And my identification card. I'm hoping, and praying, that they'll be returned to me.
(MIKE *puts them in his pocket*)

MIKE   I'll be leaving now. (*To* ANN) I count that what's transpired here will forever be unspoken.

DAVID   We promise.
(*He looks at* ANN. *There is no response from her*)

MIKE   You promise. I've heard nothing from your wife.

DAVID   Promise him, darling. Say something.

ANN (*Finally*)   Let me see that identification card.

(*The men exhale, almost too noticeably. They know they have succeeded*)

MIKE   I'm afraid you cannot see the identification card.

ANN (*Slowly*)   That's what I thought.

MIKE   It's against regulations.

DAVID   It's not allowed, Ann.

ANN (*She nods knowingly*)   You had me for a minute. Revolvers, agents with Italian haircuts, it was coming so thick and fast I didn't have time to think.

DAVID   Ann! Don't say you still don't believe me!

ANN (*Going to the closet*)   Believe you! Why a child of six would have seen through it! I don't know what took me so long!

28

MIKE I couldn't love a woman who trusted me so little.

ANN (*Taking coats out, to pack*) Oh, come on, boys. Amateur night. You're not even doing it well!
     (DAVID *strides over to* MIKE *and takes the card from his hand. He puts it on the table*)

DAVID Ann! I'm asking you not to look at this card! (*He walks away from it*) I'm begging you!

ANN (*Smiling*) Why? Because it's your driver's license?

DAVID Trust me!

ANN You're going to bluff until the end?

DAVID If you look at that card you'll be ashamed of yourself as long as you live!

ANN (*Stopping. Simply*) I'd bet my life that's not an F.B.I. card. (DAVID *folds his arms. He's as far from the card as she is. She walks to it, looking at the men's expressions. She walks slowly, confidently. She stops, measuring the distance*) Aren't you going to jump for it?

MIKE Don't do it, Ann. You'll be sorry.
     (*They don't move. She looks from one to the other, rattled. She runs to the card and grabs it. She utters a small scream and throws it back on the table.* DAVID *hangs his head in sorrow, disappointed.* MIKE *goes for his coat, sighing.* ANN *looks at them, stricken.* MIKE *goes to the table and takes the card, never looking at her*)

MIKE Good-bye, David.

DAVID 'Bye, Mike.

ANN   How could I have known? (*The men say nothing*) I'll never forgive myself, David. Will you ever forgive me?

DAVID (*Sad*)   Oh, I forgive you.

MIKE   You'll be hearing from me.

DAVID   Okay.

MIKE   Probably not from me. Someone from the bureau, I guess.

ANN (*To* MIKE)   I apologize for the things I called you.

MIKE   Forget it.

ANN   I had no right to call you those names.

MIKE   The way I look at it, it's a compliment. After all, I want people to think I'm a flighty, irresponsible—(*He remembers the word*) libertine.

ANN (*Earnestly*)   They do, they do.

MIKE   Thank you. (*Abruptly*) So long, boy!

ANN   Oh, David!
(ANN *runs into* DAVID's *arms.* MIKE *puts his hands to his ears and wigwags, grinning.* ANN *turns,* MIKE *resumes his previous appearance, not a moment too soon. A small half salute, and he's out.* ANN *clings to* DAVID, *her head on his chest*)

ANN   I'll never doubt you again as long as I live.
(ANN *is biting her trembling lower lip. Her eyes are moist*)

DAVID   Now, now. There's nothing to cry about.

ANN   (*Clinging harder*)   Hold me! Hold me!
(*He holds her. She takes him by the arm and pulls him
to the easy chair. She pushes him into it, and circles him
admiringly*)

ANN   My darling. What you must have gone through!

DAVID   Oh, now. Let's not exaggerate.

ANN   What dangers! What risks you must have run!

DAVID   No, no. A lot of it's pretty dull.

ANN   You're only saying that so's not to frighten me.

DAVID   No. You've seen too many movies. Most of it's routine.
Really.

ANN   (*She sits on his lap*)   Mmmmmm.

DAVID   You're shivering!
(ANN *buries her face in his shoulder, not wanting to be
seen. She clings to him tighter.* DAVID *smiles tentatively.
This isn't bad*)

DAVID   You're never to pump me about what I've had to do,
dear. I'm not allowed to tell.
(ANN *shivers ecstatically*)

ANN   No. I won't.

DAVID   And you're not to think of me as a hero. (*He thinks for
a moment, rocking with her. Then, since he's only human—*)
Ann?

ANN   Yes?

DAVID   If anything happens to me, dear, I'd like to be buried in
Arlington Cemetery.
   (*She trembles visibly, tightening her clinging. He smiles
   happily*)

The lights black out

SCENE FOUR

The upper left-hand corner of the stage reveals part of an office of the New York division of the Federal Bureau of Investigation.

Behind the desk is ROBERT DOYLE; *fifty, tough, competent. He is speaking on the telephone.*

DOYLE (*On phone*) That'll be all right . . . send us a copy for our files. Federal Bureau of Investigation . . . Empire State Building. Thank you.
    (*He hangs up.* HARRY POWELL *enters. He is about* DOYLE'*s age, but a bit softer*)

POWELL You send for me, Bob?

DOYLE Yeah, Harry. (*He takes a card from his desk, looks at it, and hands it over*) Citizen David Williams had an F.B.I. card printed. Why? What did Citizen Williams do with it? (*He looks off*) Mr. Schultz! (SCHULTZ *enters*) You give him the rest of the information. And we're much obliged.

SCHULTZ It might be nothing, but when the card wasn't on the TV program—

DOYLE You did the right thing, Mr. Schultz. Thank you very much.

SCHULTZ You're welcome.
    (*He exits*)

33

WHO WAS THAT LADY I SAW YOU WITH?

DOYLE Oh, Harry.

POWELL (*To* SCHULTZ, *off*) I'll be right with you.

DOYLE (*To* POWELL) Are we eating dinner at your house to-night?

POWELL (*He nods*) You want to play bridge or go to a movie?

DOYLE I don't care. The women have probably decided anyway!

(*The men smile ruefully at each other.* POWELL *exits.* DOYLE *reaches for the telephone to start another call*)

The lights black out

Eleven A.M. DAVID's *office.* DAVID, *busy with papers at his desk, is whistling happily. The door opens, admitting* MIKE.

MIKE   Hi. What do you hear from J. Edgar Hoover?
(*He shoots a cap pistol;* DAVID *jumps*)

DAVID   Cut that out. Somebody'll hear you.

MIKE   You're not a bad little actor. How'd you like to go on TV sometime?

DAVID   No, thanks.

MIKE   You know what I was thinking? I could use that plot again, for one of my shows.

DAVID   No, for Pete's sake!

MIKE   I could change it around. Set it in London. Instead of making the husband an F.B.I. man he could belong to Scotland Yard.
(*He has been looking at a half-filled beaker and now picks it up to smell it*)

DAVID   What's the matter with you? Ann watches that damned program! She'd catch on in a minute!

MIKE   O.K., keep your pants on. (*Having smelled the beaker*) Changed to a bourbon base, eh? (*Holds up the colorless liquid*) This is a hell of an idea. We could market this stuff.

35

Be a big demand from sneak drinkers who don't want people to know they're drinking. There's money in it.
(*He would drink*)

DAVID (*Calm*)   There's poison in it.
(MIKE *stops, the last possible second, spraying the few drops that are in his mouth*)

MIKE   What the hell do you keep it out for?

DAVID   What the hell do you drink it for? (MIKE *puts it down*) You keep drinking everything you see in a chemistry lab you're not going to last very long.

MIKE   Where are those girl students who want to be changed from morning to afternoon classes, and feel grateful about it? I thought I'd help you out.

DAVID   Don't be funny.

MIKE   Nothing's going to be as funny as your wife last night. (*He shakes his head at the recollection, smiling*) You know the part I liked best? When she was apologizing to me! (*He laughs*) She had tears in her eyes! I could hardly keep from busting out laughing!
(*He laughs again, too loudly.* DAVID *eyes him*)

DAVID (*Some vague loyalty to* ANN *is involved here*)   It wasn't that funny.

MIKE (*Aglow*)   You know what we ought to do now?

DAVID   What?

MIKE   Send a fake F.B.I. man up there and put her through the wringer.

DAVID No!

MIKE Be a lot of laughs.

DAVID Will you let well enough alone!

MIKE (*Reflecting*) I could get an actor to do it. And it would be another detail in case she ever got suspicious.

DAVID She's not suspicious! And I don't want anyone to go see her!

MIKE (*Unimpressed, he shakes his head*) This whole thing's unfinished. It doesn't do me credit. It's unworkmanlike.

DAVID I'm warning you, Mike, no tricks! Quit it!

MIKE There's an end dangling. It has to be rounded off.

DAVID What end's dangling?

MIKE Are you in, or are you out of the F.B.I.? That's unfinished!

DAVID I'm out!

MIKE That's not how we left it. (*Recalling*) Somebody was going to show up at your place—

DAVID (*Suddenly*) Holy mackerel! That reminds me!
(*He starts to pull off his shoe and sock*)

MIKE What's the matter?

DAVID In the middle of the night I felt somebody poking around my feet. I opened one eye. It was Ann! I said, "What are you doing down there?" She says, "I want to see the green dots again!" She's sentimental about them! Well, I'd taken a bath

37

before I went to bed and I wasn't sure they were there, so I wouldn't untuck my legs. Well, we got to wrestling around and I got her mind off the subject, but in the morning I looked, and sure enough, they were gone! I'm going to get them tattooed on. Where do you get tattooed?

MIKE (*A moment's thought*) There are places on Third Avenue. Are you sure we put those dots on your right foot?

DAVID I think so. (*He tries to remember. He looks at each foot, lifting them tentatively*) I can't remember! (*Fearful*) Ann'll remember! What'll I do?

MIKE Tattoo 'em both.

DAVID (*Relieved*) Yeah. Sure. That'll do it.
(*The phone rings*)

DAVID (*Into phone*) Hello . . . (*Real warm*) Hello, Ann, baby doll. I've been thinking of you, too . . . Of course I'm glad you called . . . I love *you* . . .

MIKE (*Waving his hand to clear the air*) Oh, brother, I can't breathe! (*He looks at his watch*) Good-bye! I'll call you later!
(DAVID *pays him no attention*)

DAVID (*Into phone*) But I did kiss you good-bye—standing in the doorway. Why doesn't that count? No—I love you the most . . .
(*He kisses into the phone as this scene blacks out and the following one lights up, the kissing overlapping in continuous action*)

Scene Six

The lights reveal ANN *in her living room, kissing into the phone.*

ANN I love you the most . . . Fellows don't know how to love like girls. You don't even know how to spell it . . . (*The doorbell rings*) The doorbell's ringing, sweetheart, probably one of the neighbors. Come home early, darling, wait until you see what I have for you . . . I mean on the stove! What's the matter with you!
(*More kisses. She hangs up and goes to the door, opening it.* POWELL *stands there. He takes his hat off*)

POWELL Mrs. Williams?

ANN Yes?

POWELL How do you do. My name is Powell . . . (*He offers an open wallet, which displays his identification card*) I'm with the Federal Bureau of Investigation.

ANN Oh, come in. Come right in, please.

POWELL (*Entering*) Thank you.

ANN (*Preceding him*) I guess I know an F.B.I. card when I see one.

POWELL You do?

ANN Won't you sit down?

POWELL Thank you.
(ANN *sits, too*)

ANN (*Crinkling her nose, and pointing to his foot*) How many dots have you? Oh, I probably shouldn't ask you that. (POWELL *is mystified*) I was just speaking to my husband when you came in.

POWELL He's not here?

ANN (*Surprised*) He's at the university!

POWELL Oh, yes. Of course.

ANN (*Earnestly*) I know why you're here, Mr. Powell.

POWELL You do?

ANN Mr. Powell, I'm going to speak sincerely to you (*Leaning forward*) I'm not like other women.

POWELL You're not?

ANN (*She shakes her head, negatively*) I can keep a secret. (*She raises her hand*) I take a sacred oath. It'll never pass my lips that David's an F.B.I. man!

POWELL Mmm.

ANN Never! I swear it! (*Suddenly*) Do you love your wife, Mr. Powell?

POWELL (*Obliged to answer*) Yes, I do.

ANN I ask you. What would you have done in a similar circumstance? I was leaving David! Divorcing him! I had my

40

reservation to Reno! He had to tell me the truth! You would have told your wife. I'm sure.

POWELL (*Fishing, waiting*) Well . . .

ANN David didn't tell me anything vital. I only know the girl that was kissing him is a foreign exchange student and the F.B.I. knows what she's up to. That's all he told me.

POWELL That's what he told you?

ANN Not another word! On my honor! (*The picture is finally clear to* POWELL. *He nods, looking at* ANN *a few moments*) Why are you looking at me like that?

POWELL Excuse me. I was just thinking that my daughter resembles you a great deal. Your eyes, and general coloring.

ANN Really?
(*He reaches into his pocket for his wallet, and shows* ANN *a picture*)

POWELL There she is, and her two little girls. They're two and three.

ANN Well, we do our hair alike. Then you're a grandfather! Why, I'd've never guessed it.

POWELL Mrs. Powell and I were married at eighteen.

ANN You don't say!

POWELL (*Pulling himself out of this*) What time does your husband come home?

ANN Six o'clock.

POWELL I'll be back then.

ANN All right. Shall I tell him that?

POWELL No, it might be better if you don't tell him anything. He might blurt out the wrong thing. Let's surprise him. Shall we?

ANN *(Smiling)* Very well.

POWELL Good-bye, Mrs. Williams.

ANN Good-bye, Mr. . . . *(She remembers)* Powell!

POWELL That's right.

ANN Don't you use other names? Like numbers? X-24?

POWELL There's no need for that here.

ANN No, I guess not. *(She crinkles her nose)* It's exciting, isn't it?

POWELL Well, it's a living.

The lights black out

Scene Seven

A telephone booth of the F.B.I. office, as in Scene 4; DOYLE *has the telephone to his ear.*

DOYLE Doyle here . . . Yes, Harry?
(*Another circle of light reveals* POWELL *at a cigar stand phone, the telephone to his ear*)

POWELL That Williams fellow with the F.B.I. card—

DOYLE Shoot.

POWELL You'll like this one. His wife caught him kissing some girl, and he told her he's an agent. He was kissing her in line of duty!

DOYLE (*Amused*) Say, why don't we try that?

POWELL (*Hesitant*) They're only kids, Bob. Hate to have it on our conscience we might break up a marriage.

DOYLE What do you suggest?

POWELL I could get hold of the husband tonight, and take him aside, and give him a hell of a lecture too.

DOYLE (*Smiling*) Okay, that'll be our good deed for today. Bring the card back.

POWELL   If I'm a little late for dinner you tell Edna I'll be right along.

DOYLE   Oke.
      (*He hangs up*)

                    The lights black out

Scene Eight

Six P.M. The WILLIAMS' *living room, deserted. The table is set for dinner for two, including a bucket cooling champagne. A smoking jacket and slippers are on and under the easy chair, a pipe and tobacco beside it on a small table.*

The door opens softly, admitting DAVID, *carrying a bouquet of roses and a small, wrapped gift box. He closes the door silently and proceeds into the room on tiptoe. He sniffs. Ah.*

He places the roses in a vase on the table and the gift on ANN'S *plate. Behind him, unseen, appears* ANN, *dressed prettily, including a trim apron. She takes in the scene, watching* DAVID *contemplate the arrangement. She smiles fondly, and tiptoes behind him, putting her hands over his eyes.*

ANN Who is it?

DAVID Well, let's see now. Give me a hint. Man, woman or child?

ANN Woman.
 (*Since* ANN *is pressed, full length, against his back, this is superfluous.* DAVID *squirms some, to be sure*)

DAVID Yes, you are. Full grown, too.

ANN Thank you.

DAVID (*He puts his arms behind him, feeling something*) Almost too full grown.
 (*She takes her arms down and slaps him until he stops*

45

her by kissing her, strongly. Still in his arms, she looks to the flowers)

ANN Thank you for the beautiful roses.

DAVID My pleasure.

ANN A present for me? (*Taking it and opening it as fast as she can*) Oh, I love presents! What is it? Tell me! (*She has it open. It's an imitation pearl necklace*)

ANN Oh! Just what I wanted, David! A pearl necklace!

DAVID They're genuine cultured pearls. As against uncultured pearls, which say "ain't."

ANN (*Delighted*) Oh, David! How did you ever think of a pearl necklace?

DAVID It's—something you're entitled to.

ANN (*Solemnly*) I'm not entitled to any more than the privilege of being married to you.

DAVID (*Embarrassed*) Now.
(*She pulls him down onto the easy chair and sits on his lap*)

DAVID Careful now! Remember what happened last night!

ANN You're not sorry, are you?

DAVID (*Through his teeth*) No, but there wasn't chicken fricassee on the stove last night.

ANN David, I'm glad everything happened as it did. I was terribly upset for a while but, altogether, it was worth it.

46

DAVID Well, if you're glad, I'm glad.

ANN I've a little confession to make.

DAVID Careful now!

ANN You know I've always loved you, just the way you are.

DAVID Thank you.

ANN And I've never felt you were a coward or anything—

DAVID Thank you.

ANN But deep down, every girl likes to think her fellow is, well, able to protect her, and fight for her, and take care of her—

DAVID Yes?

ANN And you didn't seem the sort who knew about guns, and jujitsu, and who knows what all. Why, just to be near you now gives me goose pimples all up and down my spine.
    (*She shivers, to show him*)

DAVID (*Slightly offended*) Well, I'm glad to give you goose pimples but I didn't think your opinion of me was that I was a sissy. What about that fist fight I had with that taxi driver last New Year's Eve?

ANN You got knocked out.

DAVID I was ahead on points until then.

ANN (*Smiling at him lovingly*) My big brave man. (*It just occurs to her*) Why didn't you use jujitsu on him?

DAVID You're not allowed to use it for personal reasons.

47

ANN Oh.

DAVID People seeing you use jujitsu might think it odd that assistant professors know it.

ANN Of course.

DAVID (*Eyeing her, with burlesque lasciviousness*) Still, there are one or two holds we're authorized to show people, in private. This one, for instance. (*He kisses her warmly. During it*) There goes the chicken fricassee.

ANN (*Throaty*) It tastes better when it's reheated.
(*They stay in the clinch. It looks as though dinner has been forgotten. The doorbell rings.* ANN *attempts to go but* DAVID *holds her*)

DAVID (*Whisper*) They'll go away.

ANN (*Pleased*) What about your chicken fricassee?

DAVID What chicken fricassee?
(*She goes to the door, straightening herself;* DAVID *stays on the couch. The door is opened. It's* MIKE)

ANN Hello, Michael.

MIKE Hi, Ann. (*He comes into the room, looks at the pearl necklace, the table for two, and smiles*) Good evening, David.

DAVID (*Watching him from the couch*) Good evening.

MIKE My, that looks cozy. (*To* ANN) I envy you, David. I don't think I've had a home-cooked meal in six months.

ANN (*Hesitant*) We were just sitting down to eat. You're welcome to join us. There's more than enough.

MIKE   No, thanks, but you're very kind. (*To* DAVID) I've come with good news. (DAVID *still just watches him*) Don't you want to hear it?

ANN   Yes!

DAVID (*Guardedly*)   What is it?

MIKE   I'm happy to inform you—that you're still in the F.B.I.!

ANN (*Pleased*)   Oh! I'm so glad!
    (DAVID *just glares at him*)

MIKE   I had a lot of talking to do, but I don't want to take all the credit. You've got a lot of friends on the board. (*To* ANN) They like him. (*To* DAVID) Haven't you anything to say?
    (MIKE *still looks at* DAVID. *Now* ANN *does also*)

DAVID (*Flat*)   Thank you.

ANN   I didn't know what to hope for. I'd never have forgiven myself if I'd been responsible for his dismissal.
    (MIKE *takes the gun out of his pocket and puts it on the table*)

MIKE   Your gun—(*Now he crosses to* DAVID *and puts the card in his back pocket*)—and card. There you are!

ANN   Thank you again, Mike. Very much.

MIKE   That's all right.

ANN (*She goes to him and kisses him*)   That's for being a good friend, the rarest thing on earth.

MIKE (*Willing to hold on*)   Well, David and I go back a long way together.

49

DAVID (*Ice*)   But I don't think we're going to be going *forward* much together!

ANN (*Delighted*)   Oh, jealous! I like that! Please stay for dinner! *Now* I mean it!

MIKE (*Smiling*)   I'm afraid not. (*A pause*) And I'm afraid David's not staying for dinner either.

ANN   He isn't? Why not?

MIKE (*Simply*)   We have an assignment. An important assignment!

DAVID (*The whole plot now clear to him*)   What!

ANN   Tonight?

MIKE   Now! As a matter of fact, we're a little late already.

DAVID (*Restrained only by* ANN's *presence*)   Well, I don't feel like going!

MIKE   What do you mean, you don't feel like it?

DAVID   You heard me!

ANN   David! What are you saying? They just forgave you today!

MIKE   You're practically on probation!

DAVID   I've got friends on the board! I'm taking a night off!

MIKE (*Explaining it to him*)   You're in no position to do anything but come along.

ANN I wouldn't think so! It'd be a fine F.B.I. if every agent stayed home when he felt like it!

MIKE She's got more sense than you have.
(DAVID *is pent up with frustration, but there's nothing he can do*)

DAVID (*To* ANN) I'll be back in half an hour! Maybe less!

MIKE (*Calm*) I wouldn't promise that.

ANN Of course not. How can you tell? What kind of an assignment is it? Is it dangerous?

MIKE It might be. It's the same assignment you interrupted when you walked in on David. Luckily, that girl didn't know you were David's wife.

ANN (*Alarmed*) You mean you're going out with girls?

MIKE Well, if you can call them "girls."

ANN Why can't you?

MIKE I don't call foreign agents "girls"! We've wired booth number four in Lee Wong's restaurant. When David and I go to the men's room, there'll be F.B.I. men listening to what they say to each other. We're hoping they say what we want to hear. (*To* DAVID) The Chief has confidence in this idea.
(DAVID *puts his head in his hands, the excessive invention sickening him*)

DAVID Ohh!

ANN You've wired a booth in Lee Wong's Chinese restaurant? The one on Forty-sixth Street?

MIKE   He's Lee Wong to you. Mr. Wong is one of the most important Nationalist China officials in America.

ANN   That short man? That meets you at the door?

MIKE   He's Madam Chiang Kai-shek's uncle!

DAVID *(Unable to restrain himself)*   Oh no! Stop talking! Shut up, already!
  (ANN *looks at him, puzzled*)

MIKE   You're right. I'm sorry. Forget what I told you, Ann!

ANN   You can trust me!

DAVID   You can't trust anybody! Not in the whole world! Let's get the hell out of here!

ANN *(Coming to him)*   David, take care of yourself. (*To* MIKE) Both of you.

MIKE   We will.

ANN *(Noticing* DAVID's *lack of a breast-pocket handkerchief)* I'll get you a handkerchief.

DAVID   I don't want a handkerchief.

ANN   Wait, I'll get you one.
  (*She goes, quickly.* DAVID *turns to* MIKE)

DAVID *(Viciously, low)*   When we get outside, you put your hands up! I'm going to knock your block off, you psychopath! That compulsion you have to invent isn't a talent, you're nothing but a goddamned liar!

MIKE (*Not at all alarmed*) Oh, shut up! I've got two sensational dames! They're a sister act and they won't separate! They'll separate with enough liquor in them. You ungrateful pup, you're in clover!

DAVID (*Through his teeth*) I don't want to be in clover! Did that ever occur to you?

MIKE What are you, a eunuch?

DAVID Yes! I am!

MIKE The hell you are! I tomcatted around with you too many years to go for this halo you're wearing! And don't think I believe that student kissing you out of gratitude story! This is your Uncle Michael you're talking to!

DAVID Can't you understand? I'm happily married! I don't care about outside women!

MIKE There's no risk involved! Your wife's not only allowing you to go out with beautiful dames, she's forcing you! You've fallen into the greatest racket any married man's ever had! Home cooking and outside romance! Why, I'm thinking of getting married myself! (*He watches* DAVID, *and sees that he's unhappy. He changes his tactics and smiles at him*) Cheer up, kid, we'll have a hell of a time. We make a great pair. I've missed operating without you. The guys I pair off with now don't have your technique. We were fabulous, or don't you remember?

DAVID Oh, Mike, that stuff's adolescent. You outgrow some things—

53

MIKE   Never!
(*They hear* ANN *returning.* ANN *carefully puts the folded handkerchief in* DAVID's *breast pocket*)

ANN   I'll be waiting up for you.

DAVID (*He's human*)   I wouldn't do that, dear. I may be a little late. (MIKE *Mephistopheles smiles*) You never can tell how these things turn out.

MIKE   No, you can't.
(ANN *kisses him*)

ANN   Take care of yourself.

DAVID   I will.

ANN (*Solemnly*)   David.

DAVID   Yes?

ANN (*Nathan Hale never said it stronger*)   If—if you're obliged —if you have to—(*Her lip quivers*) whatever you do—

DAVID (*Touched*)   Oh, Ann!

ANN   Just never tell me! Never let me know! (*Even* MIKE *is impressed. She throws her arms around* DAVID *and kisses him*) Go on! (*She opens the door;* MIKE *and* DAVID *go. She closes the door and leans against it, dramatically. She walks around the room, thinking. She turns the champagne bottle upside down. She sits on the sofa and spies the gun on the coffee table. Seeing it, she's galvanized into action. She picks up the gun looks at it a moment, and rushes to the door. As she opens it, she sees* POWELL, *who has just reached it. For a mo-*

ment he stands frozen, facing a woman with a gun, and in a quick movement snatches his own from the holster. They stand facing each other, guns in hand) Oh, Mr. Powell! You're late!

POWELL Lady, don't ever open a door pointing a gun unless you mean to shoot. People shoot back.
(ANN *turns and runs to the window and looks down.* POWELL *comes into the room, quite bewildered*)

ANN They're just getting into a cab! They're gone! (*She turns from the window, facing* POWELL, *pointing the gun at his stomach*) He left his gun!
(POWELL *hastily pushes it aside*)

POWELL Lady!

ANN (*She puts the gun down*) I guess you're right.

POWELL Now where is your husband?

ANN He's on an assignment. He couldn't even eat his dinner.

POWELL An assignment?

ANN Didn't you know it? Don't they tell you those things?

POWELL (*Annoyed*) Not always.

ANN I don't understand that. It doesn't seem very efficient.

POWELL I've been on a few assignments all day myself. I haven't been back to the office.

ANN I see. Well, Mike and David are having dinner at Lee Wong's with two girls they're trying to get things out of.

POWELL (*Nodding*) I'll bet.

ANN Booth number four. The booth has been wired.

POWELL It has?

ANN Oh yes. Well, Lee Wong—you know—Nationalist China—

POWELL (*Uncertain*) Yes—

ANN Well, that's all they told me. They don't tell me everything.

POWELL They tell you enough!
(POWELL *is thinking. There is quite a pause*)

ANN What are you thinking about, Mr. Powell?

POWELL (*Trace of bitterness*) I've been thinking the resemblance between you and my daughter is getting fainter all the time!

ANN What are you going to do?

POWELL Do about what?

ANN The gun! David ought to have his gun.

POWELL The gun's not the problem. The problem's my stomach!

ANN Your stomach?

POWELL I have an ulcer, Mrs. Williams. And I have to eat regularly. Reasonably regularly. I've had no lunch today. My stomach is killing me!

ANN   Oh, you poor man.
(POWELL *reflects for a moment, disgusted*)

POWELL   What's the name of that restaurant?

ANN   Lee Wong's. On Forty-sixth Street.

POWELL   (*He thinks*)   They ought to be there in twenty minutes. I'll get him on the phone. (*Not too courteously*) May I?

ANN   Certainly! (*He dials*) Shall I leave the room? (*He merely looks at her, waiting for his party to answer*) I mean if it's secret, I don't mind leaving.

POWELL   (*Into phone*)   Edna, I'll be late again . . . I don't know, not too long . . .When Bob comes tell him there's been a little hitch, and start dinner without me if you have to . . . I can't help it, dear . . . Yes, I had lunch . . . I feel fine . . . 'Bye, dear.
(*He hangs up. He looks at* ANN, *mad. He walks to a chair and sits.* ANN *also sits, watching him. A pain in the abdomen strikes him. He pokes it with his finger, grimacing. He reaches into his pocket and takes out a roll of Tums. He breaks two out of the package and puts them in his mouth, chewing them*)

ANN   Aren't they Tums?

POWELL   That's right.

ANN   Shouldn't they be eaten after dinner?

POWELL   (*Bitterly*)   Yes, they should be, Mrs. Williams! They certainly should be!
(*There is a moment of silence*)

57

ANN May I suggest something, Mr. Powell? (*He waits*) Can you eat chicken fricassee? It's not highly seasoned. I'm a very simple cook. Please eat David's dinner. It's only going to waste.

POWELL No, I couldn't do that. I—

ANN You shouldn't starve yourself. That's the worst thing for an ulcer.

POWELL Yes, it is.

ANN (*Pleased*) Not another word. You sit down to the table and I'll have food in front of you in two minutes.

POWELL That's very kind of you, Mrs. Williams. You know something? You're beginning to resemble my daughter again.

ANN Well, if we of the F.B.I. don't help each other, I'd like to know who will?

POWELL Say, that's right.
    (ANN *exits into the kitchen, while* POWELL *takes his top-coat off and sits at the table.* ANN *comes out carrying a steaming casserole, wearing heat-proof gloves. She places it on the asbestos pad of the table*)

ANN It's steaming hot. Don't burn yourself.

POWELL My, it certainly smells good.

ANN Do you like tea or coffee? Now or later?

POWELL Tea, if it's not too much trouble. And later.

ANN Well, there's boiling water on the stove, and the tea bags are right beside it. You help yourself.

POWELL   Aren't you eating?

ANN   No.

POWELL   Have you had your dinner?

ANN   I'm going to that Chinese restaurant and get this gun to David.

POWELL   Now there's no use doing that!

ANN   Oh yes, there is! He may need it.

POWELL   Mrs. Williams, he won't need any gun in that restaurant! And that's final!

ANN   Don't excite yourself, Mr. Powell. You're in an acid condition.
(She goes to the clothes closet for her coat. She puts the gun in her purse. POWELL *takes out his Tums, breaks off two, puts them in his mouth, and chews them)*

ANN   You took two a few minutes ago.

POWELL   Yes, I did!

ANN   They're not a substitute for food.

POWELL *(Bitterly)*   No, they're not, Mrs. Williams!

ANN   I'd advise you to take better care of your ulcer.

POWELL   My ulcer can damn well take care of itself! Come on, Mrs. Williams. What's the name of that restaurant again?
(Angry, he opens the door for her)

ANN   Lee Wong.

POWELL   Lee Wong!
    (*He starts to follow her out, but she turns back, halting him*)

ANN   You know, Madam Chiang Kai-shek's uncle!
    (*She turns and exits. He breathes heavily and follows her*)

The lights black out

Scene Nine

A stylized version of a small off-Broadway Chinese restaurant. Two booths, slightly angled toward each other, are right and left. Only the left booth is lighted at the moment. Two pagoda-shaped phone booths are extreme right and left. A stair way leads to an upstairs anteroom to a lounge, which has a wall phone.

The center doors, rear, open, and LEE WONG, *sixty, dressed in Chinese fashion, leads* MIKE *and* DAVID *to the booth. A young Chinese waiter accompanies them, and holds the table aside for easier seating.*

MIKE (*Looking around and at his watch*) They'll be along any minute.

WONG (*Strong Chinese accent*) Not see you long time, Misser Williams!

DAVID Well, you know how it is, Wong. I don't eat out much any more.

WONG (*Smiling*) Oh, Wong know how it is. Sad story. When man single he come here with girl often. Chinese restaurant very romantic. Pretty soon man and girl get married. Goodbye, Wong! Come only on wedding anniversary. On wedding anniversary Wong treat drinks. Wong lose money. Sad story.

DAVID I never thought of it that way, Wong.

WONG When Mrs. Williams come I bring her to booth.

61

DAVID Ah, it's—not Mrs. Williams. She's not coming. (*Embarrassed*) She couldn't come. These are old friends from school.
(WONG, *disappointed in him, nods*)

MIKE Four Missionaries' Downfalls.

WONG My house is your pleasure.
(*He goes*)

DAVID Why the hell did we have to come here? Couldn't you figure out a place where nobody knew us?

MIKE Operating in the open is the beauty of this scheme, and what's safe about it.

DAVID (*Unhappy*) There's going to be a hitch. I smell it.

MIKE You smell wrong. It's foolproof. (*The girls enter, dressed alike. Remaining in the doorway area, they adjust their clothes.* MIKE *looks straight ahead, supposedly in the mirrored, far wall. He spies the girls*) Here they come! Look in the mirror! See them! Look at those legs! Those dames are really assembled! Get those moving parts! (*Concealed facial movement*) Arrrrrrruph! Bow wow!
(*He gets up and turns to greet them as they are led to the table by Wong. The girls are* GLORIA *and* FLORENCE. *They do have great legs. Both are blondes out of bottles. They support themselves almost entirely by their singing*)

WONG (*Directly to* DAVID) Your friends from school.
(*He goes*)

FLO Have we kept you waiting?

MIKE (*Practiced exuberance*) No, not a minute! We just got here! Gloria, I want you to meet Dave Williams! Dave, this is Gloria!

GLORIA (*Big smile*) Hello, Dave.

DAVID (*Reasonable smile*) Hello, Gloria.

MIKE And her sister, Flo, my date, keep your dirty hands off her!

FLO Hi, Dave.

DAVID Hello, Flo.

MIKE You now know the Coogle sisters, and your life is about to begin. I told him all about you.

DAVID Yes, he's told me a great deal about you.

GLORIA Well, shame on him! (*This seems the right provocative note. All smile. The girls sit*) Cookies! (*She reaches for one, remembers, and puts it back*) Oh, I have to be careful what I swallow today. I was poisoned last night.

DAVID (*Making conversation*) Really?

GLORIA I ate some lousy tuna fish (*Indicating the cleavage*) It's stuck right here!

MIKE That tuna fish knows what it's doing!
　　　(*The girls laugh*)

MIKE   David, I haven't told you the truth why I set this date up between you and the Coogle sisters.

DAVID (*Eyeing him*)   Between me and the Coogle sisters?

MIKE   I know you don't like mixing business and pleasure. But I felt I owed it to these girls. And I believe I'm doing you a favor at the same time.

FLO   That's sweet of you to put it that way.

MIKE   I met these girls when they were trying out for Ted Mack's Amateur Hour.

FLO   Mr. Mack wouldn't put us on.

GLORIA   He said we didn't look like amateurs.

MIKE (*For their mutual enjoyment*)   What do you think of that?

DAVID (*The only way he can transmit his opinion of the girls*) They don't look like amateurs to me either.

GLORIA   Oh, thank you!

MIKE   Now I didn't promise the girls anything definite. Did I, girls?

FLO   No. Nothing definite.

MIKE   I merely said my best friend is vice president at CBS and he uses girls. You do use girls, don't you?

DAVID   Sometimes.

64

GLORIA He thought you might use us.

MIKE I couldn't put it better myself.

FLO We're very versatile. We sing and dance.

MIKE Like rabbits. (*The waiter comes with four drinks*) Right here!

FLO What is it?

MIKE An Oriental drink. Very tasty. Bring another round. We don't want to spoil this rhythm!

DAVID No. It's the starting and stopping that makes all the trouble with drinking! It's a shock to your nervous system.

GLORIA I never heard that.

MIKE Oh, yes. Steady drinking's the safest!

DAVID Now, what exactly have you got in mind to do with the Coogle sisters?

MIKE Well, D.W., frankly, a number of things. How would you feel about their doing commercials for the Simmons Mattress Company?

DAVID I see.

MIKE How does that appeal to you, D.W.?

DAVID I see it in my mind's eye.

MIKE Why don't we sleep on it?

DAVID   No, you just sleep on it. It's your department.

MIKE   He's very cautious. Has to be, in his position.

FLO   Well, here's looking through you.

DAVID   To absent friends, wherever they are.
(*The lights dim out on them and rise on the right booth.*
ANN *is being shown to it by* WONG, *with* POWELL *right
behind.*

WONG (*Disturbed*)   Here you are, Mrs. Williams.

ANN   Shame on you, Wong. Telling me there was no table. An
old customer like me.

WONG   I didn't see it. I thought the place was filled.

ANN   You didn't want me to see my husband here! (WONG *is
startled*) Don't worry about it. Mr. Powell's an F.B.I. man!
(POWELL *doesn't like this*)

POWELL   Now look here—you don't have to tell the whole
restaurant!

ANN   Oh, he can know! Him?

WONG   Please, Mrs. Williams, no trouble!

ANN   It's all right, Wong. (*She sits*) Before you do anything
else, please bring whatever soup you have ready in the kitchen.
Right now! Mr. Powell has an ulcer and he needs something
in his stomach!

POWELL (*Annoyed*) Oh—for heaven's sake— (*He splutters, then accepts the situation*) Would you? And some bread. Any kind.

WONG No bread in Chinese restaurant. Sorry.

POWELL Well, the soup then! Quick, please!

WONG Right away, sir.
(*He backs off and leaves*)

ANN You don't have to conceal you're an F.B.I. agent from Wong. He's one of the most important Nationalist China officials in this country.

POWELL Is that so?

ANN Didn't you know that?

POWELL I didn't know you knew.

ANN (*Peering into mirror*) Look! You can see them in the mirror!

POWELL (*Looking too*) Where?

ANN There! Look at those women! Who'd suspect it! (*Moving back*) We don't want them to see us yet. You know what I'm waiting for?

POWELL What?

ANN For David and Mike to go to the men's room.

POWELL Really?

67

ANN   They'll be going, you know.

POWELL   It's possible.

ANN   Well, the booth is wired, they want those women to talk. Didn't you know that either?

POWELL   I knew some of it.

ANN   Then, when the boys go to the men's room, you go, too, and you can slip the gun to him there.

POWELL   That seems logical. I'll wait until they go and join them in the men's room.

ANN   Isn't this exciting? (POWELL *doesn't seem excited*) I guess not to you, though. This is just another day's work, isn't it?

POWELL   No, today's been a little different.
       (WONG *brings the soup and a plate of cookies*)

ANN   That was very quick, Wong.

POWELL   I'm much obliged.
       (WONG *nods*)

ANN   I'll have chicken chow mein, Wong.

POWELL   And can I have some scrambled eggs? Soft? (WONG *bobs and leaves.* POWELL *quickly takes a sip. He looks at the plate of cookies*) What are they?

ANN   Cookies. (*He takes a handful, crumples them, and puts them in the soup, stirring them with the spoon*) It's going to be awful sweet.

POWELL   It's starch! I'm supposed to eat starch!
(*He is about to dip his spoon in again, but something
in the soup stops him*)

ANN   What's the matter?

POWELL   Those little papers!

ANN   Oh, they're fortune cookies! You should have taken out
the fortunes first. (*She takes a spoon*) Here, let me help you.
(*They both fish. She reads one from the spoon*) "Adventure
is just around the corner." What do you think of that?
(POWELL *has taken out a couple with his spoon and now
gives up in impatience*)

POWELL   (*Taking a spoonful of soup*)   Ah, the hell with it!
They must be starch!
(DAVID's *booth lights up.* ANN's *booth remains lighted*)

MIKE   Tell me, David, what are you doing about the Lucky
Strike program?

DAVID   Frankly, I haven't decided. I've been thinking of cancel-
ing it.

MIKE   (*To the girls*)   He's got a lot of problems.

GLORIA   I would think so.

MIKE   I hope you're not heading for a crack-up, boy.

DAVID   (*Belittling*)   Oh, I'm all right.

MIKE   You take care of yourself. You don't want to have a
nervous breakdown.

69

DAVID I relax every once in a while. I'm relaxing now.

MIKE You know what you ought to do? In my opinion?

DAVID What?

MIKE You ought to go away for a week end. Say in Atlantic City?

DAVID (*Out of the assumed character*) How the hell could I go away for a week end?

MIKE (*Meaningly*) On an assignment.
(The waiter comes with a new round of drinks)

ANN (*Staring straight ahead, into the mirror*) They're giving them more drinks. (*Pleased*) Get them drunk, David! Go on! (POWELL *looks into the mirror*) They're doing a good job, aren't they?

POWELL They're a credit to the bureau.

ANN I'm proud of them. Those girls are going to be talkative all right. I wonder when the boys are going to the men's room?
(POWELL notices that both boys have their glasses to their lips)

POWELL Pretty soon, now.
(The waiter has finished serving the new drinks to DAVID's foursome and taken the old glasses. He leaves)

FLO Want to powder your nose?

GLORIA I don't think so.

70

FLO (*Oddly adamant*)   Yes you do!
(GLORIA *looks at her, sees the expression*)

GLORIA   Well, if you say so.
(*The men rise, making room for them to leave*)

ANN (*Alarmed*)   Oh! Look who's going to the men's room!
I mean the ladies' room! I'm going to slip David the gun!
(*She reaches for her purse, but* POWELL *puts his hand on it*)

POWELL   No ma'am! (ANN *looks at him for an explanation*)
Someone might see you pass it. It's too risky.

ANN   I'll tell them you're here! It'll make them feel better!

POWELL   Yes, do that. That'll make them feel better!
(ANN *goes to the rear.* DAVID *and* MIKE, *having waited for the girls to leave the table, now seat themselves*)

MIKE   What do you think? How we doin', boy?

DAVID   Oh, brother, your standard's gone down. And what's that week end bit?

MIKE   Why not? Let's make it something. We'll get one of those three-room suites with a living room in the middle— (*He gestures with both hands, clearly indicating the girls swishing back and forth*) wissh wissh! Play crisscross! Like we used to do! What do you say? Lots of laughs!

DAVID (*He shakes his head*)   Nope.

MIKE   What's the matter with you anyway? Where's your old zing? You hitting premature middle age?

DAVID (*He sighs heavily*) Half the attraction of being out on the town is that it's forbidden. All I can think of is how Ann looked when we left. "If you have to," she said. "Just never let me know!" She actually gave me permission! She sent me! With tears in her eyes! How the hell can a man enjoy that kind of cheating! She's ruined it for me!
(ANN's *head pops up from behind the booth*)

ANN Pssst! (*The boys are startled at her presence.* ANN *speaks low, tensely*) Keep calm! Don't look around! There's an F.B.I. man in the booth across! He missed you at the apartment! He's watching everything!
(*She ducks her head, disappearing*)

DAVID What the hell was that? An F.B.I. man! (*Suddenly occurring to him*) Did you send an actor to my place? Why, you stupid idiot! I'll break your damned neck! I'll—
(*He's speechless*)

MIKE (*Dazed*) I didn't send any actor!

DAVID You didn't?
(*They both look around, bewildered*)

MIKE I didn't send anyone! I swear to God!
(POWELL *never stops watching them in the mirror. They look, by swiveling their eyes, fearful, trying to give the impression they're not scanning the place. The upstairs anteroom lights up, revealing* FLO *dialing,* GLORIA *beside her.* DAVID, *searching the room, finally looks in the mirror and sees* POWELL. *Their eyes meet.* POWELL *nods, grimly, admitting his identity*)

DAVID   Oh no!

MIKE   What's the matter?

DAVID   (*Not moving his lips*)   There he is! In the mirror! (MIKE *sees* POWELL. *He, too, is frozen.* POWELL *merely looks at them*) I'm sick!
> (*He and* MIKE *try vainly to hide their heads, while still peering at* POWELL)

FLO   (*Into phone*)   Hello, Al? . . . This is Flo Coogle . . . I hate to call you at home, Al, but this is kind of an emergency . . . Well, you're our agent, ain't you? We need advice!. . . We're with two guys. One's a writer from CBS, Mike Haney, and the other says he's a vice president . . . David Williams . . . They're talking about a job, but they're throwing in Atlantic City!
> (POWELL *catches* DAVID's *eye, motions him to leave*)

DAVID   Mike, he wants us to leave. (POWELL *mouths "You go home"*) He wants me to go— (*Also mouthing it*) —home!

MIKE   (*Calling*)   Waiter, we want to pay the check!
> (ANN *reappears through the center doors and hurries up the left stairs. Unobserved, she listens to* FLO's *phone conversation*)

FLO   (*Into phone*)   Okay . . . (*Hard*) Okay, you told me enough!
> (*She hangs up*)

GLORIA   (*Low voice, intense*)   Well?

FLO   (*Still hard*)   We weren't wrong. How could we've been so stupid? He says get rid of 'em! Just get rid of 'em!

GLORIA   The dirty rats!

FLO   I could kill them with my bare hands!

GLORIA   With pleasure!

FLO   Oh, we'll take care of them! Or my name isn't Florence Coogleofsky!

GLORIA   Oh!
(ANN *is horrified at what she's heard. She races down the stairs and over to* POWELL)

ANN   They know who the boys are! They're going to kill them!

POWELL (*Startled*)   Who is? What is?

ANN   I heard them in the ladies' room! They called somebody on the telephone! They were told to "get rid of them"!

POWELL (*Putting his fork down*)   Now speak slowly! Calmly!

ANN (*Sitting on the edge of the booth seat, no calmer*)   Those girls, they were given orders to get rid of the boys, and they're going to kill them! Stop them! Stop them!

POWELL   Now there's no reason to get excited—

ANN (*Louder*)   Didn't you hear me?

POWELL   Sssh! Lower your voice! We've got everything under control. The F.B.I.'s a very efficient organization—

ANN   You didn't hear the phone call! It just happened!

POWELL (*As though talking to a child*)   Shh! Don't worry about it. Everything's arranged. We're going to finish our eggs, quietly, and then we're going back to your apartment, where your husband will be waiting for us. I'm going to have a little private talk with him, and then I'll leave you, and you two can have a nice evening together. You see, this is your husband's last day with the F.B.I. We feel he's done enough. (FLO *and* GLORIA *start back to the booth downstairs*) Now, if you'll excuse me, I'll phone my wife and tell her I'll be a little late.

    (*He goes to the pagoda phone booth, right*)

ANN But, Mr. Powell—

DAVID (*As the girls approach*) There's no use sitting down! We're leaving!

FLO Leaving? What for? We haven't eaten!

MIKE He just got a call from CBS. He has to hurry right over. It's an emergency.

GLORIA What kind of emergency?

MIKE A tube blew out.
    (*Throwing money on the table, they start hustling the girls out*)

POWELL (*On phone*) Hello, Edna . . . I'll be late again—

ANN Mr. Powell, they're leaving! Aren't you going to stop them?

POWELL Sssh! It's all right.

ANN (*Fumbling in her purse for the gun*) I'll stop them!
    (*She has the gun out, and runs*)

75

POWELL Holy—(*He drops the phone and chases her off stage, through the center doors. There is a hubbub offstage. A shot rings out. Another. Three more in succession. More hubbub.* POWELL *staggers in, his coat half off, revealing a blood-stained arm, which he clutches. He goes back to the telephone booth*) Aaaaah! (*Into phone*) Edna! Put Bob on the phone! Quick! . . . Bob, send a car to Wong's Chinese restaurant, Forty-sixth, west of Broadway! I've been hit, not bad. Williams' wife had a gun. I tried to get it from her, it went off! It's the goddamnedest mix-up you ever saw! A crowd's collecting. We better get 'em the hell out of here! What . . . ?

> (*He turns into booth, to continue his conversation, as* JOE BENDIX, *who has entered in a rush during the phone conversation, begins to speak in the pagoda phone booth, left*)

BENDIX (*On phone*) City desk! Bendix here! I fell into the damnedest story! I was walking by Wong's Chinese restaurant, Forty-sixth, west of Broadway, when a gun went off, not ten feet from me! It hit somebody, I don't know who yet, but you better take as much of the story as I got! (*He refers to his pad*) The woman who fired the gun is Mrs. David Williams. First she thought she'd hit her hsuband, and she got pretty hysterical. (POWELL *hangs up and starts out slowly*) I got the story in snatches, but here's the important part! Her husband's an F.B.I. man, he's been an undercover F.B.I. man for years . . . (POWELL *stops in horror, then starts for* BENDIX) And he's a plain, ordinary assistant chemistry professor at Columbia University!

POWELL You can't print that! Hang up the phone!

BENDIX (*Struggling to keep* POWELL'S *hand away from the phone*)   Get the hell away!

POWELL   You can't print that story!

BENDIX (*Into phone*)   I'm fighting some nut, Chief! Send people! (*Using his knee on* POWELL)   Get the hell away from me!

(WONG *and the waiter enter and join in, shouting in Chinese, as*

The curtain falls

ACT TWO

ACT TWO

SCENE ONE

The F.B.I. office, now looking considerably lived in. Empty milk bottles, waxed paper, and coffee cartons bespeak the vigil. Opened newspapers are about. The occupants are listening to a radio broadcast. They are DOYLE, *grim;* POWELL, *bandaged;* EVANS, *a new F.B.I. man, younger than the others; a* SECRETARY; *and* MIKE, *quite, quite subdued.*

THE RADIO VOICE *(Heard as the curtain rises)* Tomorrow's head-lines today! The midnight edition of the news, happenings at home and abroad, broadcast each evening at this time through the courtesy of Seeley's Epsom Salts, tones your system while you sleep.

ANOTHER VOICE Just a few short hours ago a pistol shot off Times Square brought home to the American people the re-minder, once again, of the role played by our never slumber-ing F.B.I. in their never ceasing vigil over the security of our country. A simple, ordinary assistant professor of chemistry at Columbia University, known to his friends and family as simple David Williams, stands revealed today as an under-cover F.B.I. agent. Quiet and unassuming, he went about his duties with an innocence his closest friends never pierced—

DOYLE *(Overlapping)* Shut it off! It's the same one they had at eleven o'clock. (EVANS, *near the set, does. Silence. Finally*

81

DOYLE *looks at* POWELL) "They're just kids, Bob. We don't want to have it on our conscience we broke up their marriage!" You and your goddamn Irish sentiment!

POWELL What are you, Italian? *You* agreed to it!

DOYLE I'm not running out on the rap! (*Bitterly, directed at himself*) Because I can't. (*To* POWELL) Oh, we're both going to get it, good! (*To the* SECRETARY) Read the last part back.

SECRETARY "On receiving the telephone call from Agent Powell that he had been shot trying to wrest the revolver from Mrs. Williams I immediately dispatched a car, hoping to spirit the principals away and avoid any undue publicity."
(*She looks at* DOYLE, *waiting for him to go on*)

DOYLE (*Glaring at* POWELL *while he dictates*) However, a juxtaposition of unfortunate circumstances worked against us. A newspaperman happened to be in the vicinity, and Mrs. Williams, in her hysteria, revealed the story. Or what she thought was the story. Our task at concealment was further complicated when a roving television news truck, assigned to the Times Square area, also arrived, and secured a fuller story from the still hysterical Mrs. Williams. (*To* EVANS) What network was it?

EVANS CBS. They interrupted a Jack Benny broadcast.

DOYLE (*Masochisticly*) I wonder how many stations that is?

MIKE One hundred and forty. (DOYLE *turns to him, eyes narrowed. Weakly*) I thought you wanted to know.

EVANS The networks are leading off their news breaks with it.

82

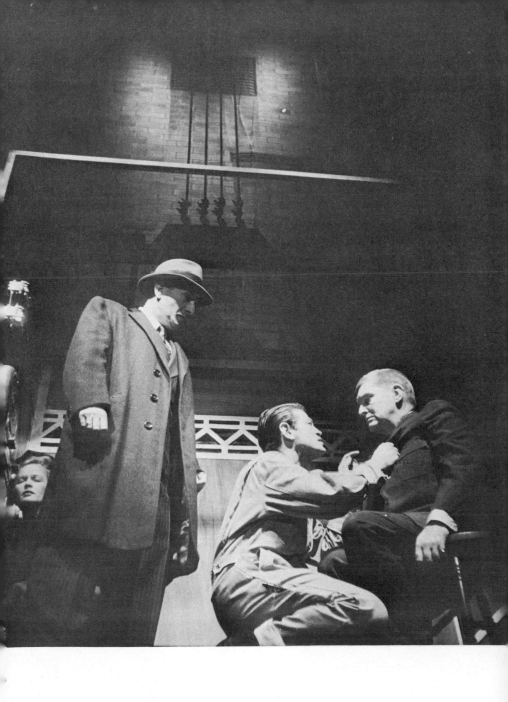

DOYLE (*Bitterly*)   What they'll do with this story tomorrow! We'll be the laughing stock of the country! Of the world! This is the stuff *Pravda* puts on the front page. With cartoons! (*He sighs. He must go on. Dictating*) We took Mr. and Mrs. Williams to their apartment, where they were cautioned against any additional statements to the press. We have stationed a man outside their door. The two Coogle women have no suspicion of their involvement, believing two other women must be the foreign agents mentioned. They were taken home and put to bed. (*He doesn't like the sound of this*) Change that to "were permitted to go to sleep." We have the other principal—(*He looks at* MIKE, *stonily*)— Michael Haney, the instigator and inventor of the impersonation, in voluntary custody. You admit it's voluntary?

MIKE   Oh, yes sir. I'm voluntary. I mean, it's voluntary.

DOYLE   Have you got an extra bed in your apartment?

MIKE   Yes sir.

DOYLE (*To* EVANS)   Have Gibson stick with him tonight. (*To* MIKE)   You're to be back here tomorrow morning at ten o'clock. And your partner with you!

MIKE   Yes sir.
(MIKE *skirts* DOYLE, *who is in his path, and exits hastily.* DOYLE *takes a deep, despondent breath. The* SECRETARY *looks at him expectantly, pencil poised*)

DOYLE (*Without confidence*)   In conclusion, may I point out it was a juxtaposition of unfortunate circumstances.

SECRETARY   Yes sir.
(*She exits*)

POWELL We ought to get some sleep. Tomorrow'll be a big day.

DOYLE That's what it'll be. Go on home.
(EVANS *and* POWELL *get up*)

POWELL What are you going to do?

DOYLE (*Looking toward the machine*) I'm going to wait for the teletype from Washington. It'll start clicking in a minute! Just about now they're a little puzzled why their files don't show any agent who's an assistant chemistry professor in Columbia University!
(*The* SECRETARY *enters*)

SECRETARY A Mr. Parker is outside. He says he's from the Central Intelligence Agency. He'd like to see you.
(*The men look at* DOYLE)

EVANS That's pretty quick.

DOYLE (*To the* SECRETARY) Send him in. (*To* EVANS *and* POWELL) C.I.A. couldn't know about it yet! I don't think! Let him do the talking!
(*The* SECRETARY *ushers in a man who complements* DOYLE; *she leaves*)

PARKER Hello, Doyle.

DOYLE Hello, Parker.

POWELL Hi, Parker.

PARKER (*He looks at the scattered newspapers*) Reading your press notices?

DOYLE What can I do for you?

PARKER Little late, isn't it? Shouldn't you have done something earlier?

DOYLE (*Alert for what* PARKER *knows*) Well, that's cryptic enough. What's bothering you?

PARKER (*Tight-lipped*) What do you think's bothering me?

DOYLE I'm trying to find out.

PARKER What the hell do you think we are? The C.I.A. is an intelligence agency just as much as you are! Keeping scientists undercover at Columbia University falls under our directive as much as it does yours! You had no right to assume it by yourself!

DOYLE Is that your beef? That we didn't let you in on it?

PARKER Yes, that's my beef!

DOYLE Well, all I can say is I'm sorry you weren't in on it with us. I'm sorry from the bottom of my heart. And I wish it wasn't too late to let you in on it now.

PARKER (*Suspicious of this generosity*) Yeah? Well, why is it too late? Maybe we *can* help on something?

DOYLE (*Sadly*) No, it's too late.

PARKER I don't think so. Where are those two women you've got? You've hidden them away someplace! Let *us* have them for a while.

DOYLE I'm afraid I couldn't do that.

PARKER (*Contemptuous*) No. Talk is cheap. You talk coördinating, but when it comes right down to it, you take all

85

the bows. (*He takes the recording from his pocket*) We've intercepted a phone call, but you don't see me keeping it to myself. I bring it over here! I coöperate!

DOYLE Parker, I tell you all this just happened. It wasn't planned.
(PARKER *gives the tape to* EVANS, *who will put it on the machine*)

PARKER (*Only slightly mollified*) Yeah. I'm sure. (*Indicating the tape*) We've been keeping a wire tap on these characters for a long time. They finally came through with a phone call half an hour ago.
(*He indicates that* EVANS *should start*)

C.I.A. VOICE Telephone conversation intercepted eleven-forty P.M. Background of speakers: Ladislov Belka, member of his country's United Nations delegation. Supposedly here in cultural capacity. Other speaker is Nicholas Orlov, known foreign agent.
(*There is silence on the tape, then the sound of a telephone ringing*)

ORLOV'S VOICE Hello.

BELKA'S VOICE This is Belka speaking!

ORLOV'S VOICE Yes, Belka?

BELKA'S VOICE Who the hell were those two women of ours the F.B.I. caught in that Chinese restaurant?

ORLOV'S VOICE I don't know, Belka! They don't belong to my group! Not mine!

BELKA'S VOICE Whose are they?

ORLOV'S VOICE I don't know. Not mine.

BELKA'S VOICE How did all this happen?

ORLOV'S VOICE It was a juxtaposition of unfortunate circumstances.

BELKA'S VOICE How can I find out who handled this?

ORLOV'S VOICE It'll take a few days. I have to check, it's not
simple—

BELKA'S VOICE I can't wait a few days! I want those doctors'
names now! Do we know anything?

ORLOV'S VOICE Only that an F.B.I. man has the information in
his head.

BELKA'S VOICE I read that in the newspapers! Come over to my
apartment!

ORLOV'S VOICE Now?

BELKA'S VOICE It may interest you to know they're quite concerned about this in Moscow!

ORLOV'S VOICE Moscow?

DOYLE *and* POWELL Moscow!

BELKA'S VOICE Yes, Moscow!
 (EVANS *stops the machine. There is a moment's silence*)

DOYLE The poor bastards!

POWELL (*Reflectively*) I've been worried about the cold war.
No more. We're not going to lose it.

DOYLE No. Tie, maybe. That's the worst we'll get.

PARKER What's the matter with you? What the hell do you care what happens to them?

DOYLE Today I've got sympathy for anybody in a jam.

PARKER Have sympathy for me! You put me in a hell of a jam! I'll tell you the truth, Doyle. This is a game two can play. I get a chance to give you the finger, I'll gladly do it!

DOYLE I'll be careful.

PARKER You can't always be careful! Or lucky! My time'll come!
  (*He exits, slamming the door*)

EVANS He's pretty mad.

DOYLE (*Flat*) He won't be tomorrow. He's in for a real good time tomorrow. Probably get hysterical. (*He shakes his head. Wistfully*) I sure would've liked to coördinate. You get two departments in on a foul-up, you split the blame. (*Earnestly*) Sometimes if you can get enough departments involved— (*Pantomiming the mound being smoothed out*) the blame gets spread so thin you can't even find it.
  (*He shakes his head again, sadly. He clutches his stomach and rubs.* POWELL *takes his roll of Tums from his pocket and hands it to him.* DOYLE *takes two and chews them. He prepares to return the roll*)

POWELL Keep it. I bought a carton.
  (*The teletype starts, all look to it*)

DOYLE There it is. (POWELL *walks to the machine.* DOYLE *starts guessing at the message*) Urgent under what name Williams listed our file answer urgent. (POWELL *is reading the message, still coming in on the machine*) Just tell me who it's from.

POWELL (*Still reading the paper coming out of the machine*) From Chief.

DOYLE (*Sadly*) I thought Hoover'd be asleep by now. Read it slowly.

POWELL (*Reading as the machine prints*) "Chief to Doyle. Keep women you have in custody isolated from each other permit no interviews am arriving tomorrow take charge personally stop congratulations on job well done."

The lights dim out

SCENE TWO

The WILLIAMS *living room,* 9 A.M. *The table is set for break-fast. It is a sunny, cheerful morning. And nobody is sunnier and more cheerful than* ANN, *who is humming happily as she cuts clippings from half a dozen papers scattered over the coffee table. She is pasting them in a scrapbook. She looks at the tele-phone, which is off its cradle, goes to it, and tentatively puts it back. It rings immediately. She picks it up quickly, sighs, puts her finger on the cradle to break the connection, and leaves it off the cradle again, returning to her humming and newspaper clippings.*

The bedroom door opens, and DAVID *enters, dressed in a bathrobe. He looks awful. He comes into the room, slowly, dragging his feet.*

ANN (*Oversolicitous*) Were you able to get any sleep, dar-ling? (*He shakes his head*) None at all? (*He shakes his head again*) I don't understand it. You took two sleeping pills.

DAVID (*Slumping into the chair*) Three.

ANN Three? That's too many!

DAVID (*His first look at her. Meaningly*) I'd have taken more! That's all there were in the bottle!

ANN (*Smiling at him*) You poor dear! You never react well to excitement! (*An intimate tone*) I remember the night we were married! (*He looks at her, wearily*) I'll get you some coffee. (*She goes. His eye falls on the newspaper headlines.*

90

He puts his face in his hands, his elbows on the table. He's not happy. ANN *comes back with the coffee*) Hot and black. I've got the nicest surprise for you for your breakfast. Guess.

DAVID   I don't feel like guessing.

ANN   Go on. Try. What would you rather have than anything in the world?

DAVID   Hemlock.

ANN (*Oblivious*)   Oh, come on. Guess.

DAVID   Don't feel like guessing.

ANN   English kippers!
    (*She is disappointed at his apathy*)

DAVID   I'm sorry, Ann. I don't feel like eating.

ANN   Not even English kippers?

DAVID   Not even English kippers.

ANN   And that nice F.B.I. man went to all that trouble.

DAVID (*Alert*)   What F.B.I. man?

ANN   The one they have outside the door, to keep reporters out. I had to promise I wouldn't unlock the door, and he went to the delicatessen and got them. (DAVID *looks at her, unbelieving*) I had to coax him. He was grumpy in the beginning. (*She sits down, cheerfully talkative*) I've been thinking, David, what *is* the purpose of the green dots on your heel? Howard didn't know.

DAVID   Who's Howard?

ANN   The F.B.I. man outside! Howard Comstock! Wake up, sleepy! (*He nods*) When two F.B.I. men meet they certainly don't take their shoes off to identify each other. The only thing I could think of would be in case of accident you could identify the corpse.

DAVID   That's what it's for.

ANN   Still, fingerprints could do that.

DAVID   I guess so.

ANN   Of course there could be circumstances where two F.B.I. men didn't have any other identification on them. Like if they were naked. I can imagine that.

DAVID (*Eyeing her*)   You can? (*She nods*) You've got quite an imagination.

ANN (*Happily*)   Do you know what I'm doing? I'm making a scrapbook so we'll always have a record of our adventure.

DAVID   Leave room for the ending.

ANN (*Indicating the newspapers*)   Oh, there won't be enough room in just one scrapbook! And these are only the morning papers! I'm going to make a lamp shade out of newspaper clippings. Won't that be a conversation piece?

DAVID (*He nods, anything*)   Yep.

ANN   I was thinking of papering the powder room with them, but I thought it might be a little— (*She crinkles her nose*) ostentatious.

DAVID   A little.

ANN (*Showing him two clippings*) Which picture of me do you like better?

DAVID (*He looks*) They're both nice.

ANN I like this one. I photograph better on my left side. (*Indicating the other*) Sylvia thinks this one is better. I'm dying to call a hundred people but I can't use the phone. I've only been able to get through to Sylvia and Mother. Watch. (*She goes to the phone and puts it back in the cradle. It rings*) See? I'll answer this one. (*Into phone*) Yes? Yes, this is Mrs. Williams . . . Oh, how do you do . . . Well, we had the receiver off the hook because so many strangers were calling up. I hope we didn't inconvenience you. (*Her hand over the mouthpiece. To* DAVID) A man from the Public Relations Department of the F.B.I. He wants to take our pictures. We're to be at the Empire State Building at four o'clock. (*Into phone*) Here's Mr. Williams now. (*She hands the phone to a reluctant* DAVID, *speaking to him from two feet away*) They want to take my picture too!

DAVID (*Listless, into phone*) Yes sir?

ANN (*Seventh heaven*) What shall I wear? My blue. No, my gray!

DAVID (*Listening*) . . . Yes sir . . .

ANN No, my blue! Blue photographs better! Thinner!

DAVID (*Listening*) . . . Yes sir . . .
   (ANN *sings, out of sheer exuberance, "Tra, la la, la la!"* DAVID *hangs up*)

ANN Four o'clock? I can do my hair! Oh, isn't this exciting?
   (ANN *exits to the bedroom.* DAVID *looks at the papers on*

*the floor, and shudders. He gets up and goes for the
liquor. He pours himself a drink.* ANN *enters*)

ANN Oh, celebrating! (DAVID *drinks*) David, I need a purse
to go with my blue suit. I have to have it.

DAVID No, you don't.

ANN But I do! The only blue purse I have is for evening, with
beads!

DAVID They're not going to photograph us!

ANN (*Puzzled*) Why not? (DAVID *looks into her face, summoning the courage to tell her all*) Why not, David?

DAVID (*Unable to say the words, turning away*) Oh, they'll call
it off by then.

ANN (*Following*) They will not! Why should they? They're
proud of you! And so am I! I don't think your modesty's becoming in this instance. No, I don't! (DAVID *slumps onto the
sofa.* ANN *continues, happily*) Sylvia's dying of envy! She's
green! And you should have heard Mother! She says she always knew there was something odd about you! She wants
us for dinner tonight.

DAVID I don't think so.

ANN It'll be buffet. You're the attraction. There'll be forty
people.

DAVID I'm not in the mood for it.

ANN I didn't promise. I said if we could.

DAVID We can't.

ANN You don't know how you'll feel by tonight.

DAVID (*Rising vehemence*) Yes, I do.

ANN How could you know?

DAVID (*Loud*) I know! I know how I'll feel! (*Contrite*) I'm sorry.

ANN (*Concerned*) What's the matter, David? (*Intuition—solemnly*) Something *is* the matter!

DAVID (*He looks at her, and makes up his mind*) Yes, something is the matter.

ANN Whatever's troubling you, I'd like to hear it. I'm your wife, I share your good as well as your bad.

DAVID I love you, Ann.

ANN And I love you, David.

DAVID Everything I've done has been motivated by my love for you. Perhaps if I'd loved you less, things would have de veloped differently.

ANN Tell me, David. Tell me everything. (*And the doorbell rings*) If Howard lets them ring it's all right. (*She opens the door, admitting* MIKE. *It's quite a subdued* MIKE) Mike darling, good morning!

MIKE (*Entering*) Good morning.

ANN (*Calling offstage*) Want another cup of coffee, Howard?

HOWARD'S VOICE (*Calling back*) No, thank you.

95

ANN (*To someone else offstage*) I'm Mrs. Williams, if no one is going to introduce us.

GIBSON'S VOICE My name is Paul Gibson.

ANN How do you do, and would you like some coffee?

GIBSON'S VOICE No, thank you.

ANN If you want anything, just ring! (*She closes the door. To* MIKE) Your F.B.I. man is nice. Was he with you all night? (MIKE *nods. To* DAVID) It's Paul Gibson. Don't you want to say hello to him?

DAVID No, I don't think so.

ANN That's not very polite.

DAVID He understands.

ANN Well—I must say you F.B.I. men behave strangely to each other. (*She looks closer at* MIKE) You look awful, Mike.

MIKE I'm no hyprocrite, that's how I feel.

ANN Didn't you get any sleep? (MIKE *shakes his head*) Neither did David.

MIKE (*To* DAVID) They want us at the F.B.I. office at ten o'clock.
(DAVID *nods, forlorn*)

ANN What were you going to tell me, David, before Mike came in. The thing that's troubling you?
(DAVID *looks at her a moment, then at* MIKE, and decides *to postpone telling her*)

DAVID Oh, just a feeling I had. That's all.

96

ANN   That you're not in the F.B.I. any more?

DAVID   That's it.

ANN   It's not your fault, David. Don't reproach yourself. Mr. Powell told me last night in the Chinese Restaurant that you weren't going to be with the F.B.I. any more.

DAVID   Is that what he said?

ANN   "You've done enough," he said. (*The men exchange glances*) So you don't have to feel badly. (*She kisses him*) Mike? (*He looks to her*) Would you be real sweet and help me in an article I'm going to write for *Good Housekeeping*. It's to be called "How It Felt To Be the Wife of an Undercover F.B.I. Agent." They're paying me a dollar a word.

MIKE   (*A long look at her*)   I've never gotten a dollar a word.

ANN   How long should I make it?

MIKE   As long as you can.

DAVID   (*Counting on his fingers*)   I didn't know my husband was an undercover F.B.I. man. That's twelve dollars. Make two words out of didn't—did not. That'll be another dollar.

ANN   Well, I'm certainly going to make it longer than that!

DAVID   (*Impelled by masochism*)   How? How can you write how it felt to be the wife of an undercover F.B.I. man if you didn't know your husband was an F.B.I. man?

ANN   I thought Mike would help me there.

MIKE   No, that's too tough. But you'll get chances to write other pieces. "How It Feels To Be the Wife of a Lifer."

97

ANN   Lifer? What's that?

MIKE (*Flat*)   Inside joke.

ANN (*Big smile, envious*)   Oh, the secrets you two have! Well, I better make the beds. We don't know who'll be here today! (*She goes.* MIKE *looks to* DAVID, *waiting for him to talk.* DAVID *finally turns to him*)

DAVID   One thing's definite! We're not going to be in the same cell together! I don't want to even be in the same prison with you! If we're in the exercise yard and we come face to face don't you talk to me!

MIKE (*Ignoring* DAVID's *speech. A flat recital*)   Ed Sullivan called me. He wants us on his program this Sunday. He'll give us fifteen hundred bucks each. All we have to do is bow and wave back. I also had a call from the head of our advertising agency. He'd like to give me a dinner and a platinum watch with diamond numerals. Could I make a little speech about my secret work in the F.B.I.? I don't have to tell too much, just unimportant things. And in future interviews can I get in a plug for our product. Like F.B.I. men drink Golden Dairy Milk!
(*Silence a moment*)

DAVID   How much trouble are we really in? Legally?

MIKE   I'm glad you asked that. (*He takes a piece of paper from his pocket*) I was curious myself, and on the way over I stopped at the library. I'm not clear on all the charges, but just adding up the federal offenses, felonies and over, counting time off for good behavior, C.O.D. Sing Sing, it comes to a hundred and eighty years.

DAVID   That seems fair. Ninety years apiece.

98

MIKE   No. That's separately.

DAVID   I thought it was a bargain. (*Silence*) What the hell are we waiting for? Why doesn't something happen?

MIKE   Something'll happen. Don't worry about it.

DAVID   I'd rather they come for me and have it over with than sit cooped up here with F.B.I. men outside the door!

MIKE   We better learn being cooped up.

DAVID   I blame you for this! We're clear on that! This is all your fault!

MIKE   My fault! Who the hell kissed that foreign exchange student? Me?

DAVID   Whose harebrained idea was it to make me an F.B.I. man? And even that wasn't the trouble! We got away with that! It was mixing me up with your goddamned Coogle sisters! That was what did it!

MIKE   (*Bitterly*)   What did it was your wife playing cops and robbers! Listening to telephone calls in ladies' rooms! Shooting guns off on Forty-sixth Street! That damned buttinski! She ought to be put the hell away!
      (ANN *enters and walks to* MIKE)

ANN   (*Sweet, sweet voice*)   Mike darling. I've got some wonderful kippers. Let me fix them for you? With scrambled eggs. What do you say? (*Nodding at him solicitously*) Please eat something. (*Searching his face*) You don't look so well, Mike. (*Tracing with her finger under his eye*) You're getting circles. You don't take care of yourself. I'm going to make you my responsibility. Until you find a nice girl to make a home for you you're going to eat here at least three nights a week. You're our best friend. Our very best friend. And we love you, Mike. (*She leans forward and kisses him on the cheek. She looks to* DAVID) Is that all right, dear?

DAVID (*Glad to turn the knife*) It's fine.

ANN (*To* MIKE) Kippers and scrambled eggs?

MIKE (*Shamefaced*) No, thanks.

The lights dim out

SCENE THREE

Ten A.M., *the same morning.*
The F.B.I. office. DOYLE *and* POWELL *sit, arms folded, silent.*
They stare ahead, just waiting.
For an interval, there is no sound or movement.

DOYLE (*Resigned voice*) Wouldn't you think someone would have caught on by now?

POWELL (*Same tone*) It's only ten in the morning. Everyone's just settling down. (*Heavily, looking at the phone*) Any minute.

DOYLE Who do you think'll find out first?

POWELL Some newspaperman. The first one that calls Columbia University'll have the story.

DOYLE No, it won't come out through Columbia. The dean called me this morning. He said he knew there was some government priority work going on in the physics department, but it was news to him we were in the chemistry building.

POWELL (*He shakes his head*) Isn't that the damnedest thing, how everyone believes that story?

DOYLE Why shouldn't they believe it? Look at a newspaper. What's going on in the world today is wilder than the pulp fiction we used to read as kids.

POWELL   You might be right.

DOYLE   I tell you, it's caught up with us. Truth's finally stranger than fiction.
   (*The door opens, admitting* EVANS *escorting* DAVID *and* MIKE)

DAVID (*Tentative*)   Good morning.

MIKE   Good morning.
   (*No answer from anyone.* DAVID *and* MIKE *sit,* DOYLE *and* POWELL *not taking their eyes from them*)

DAVID   Aren't we entitled to a lawyer?

DOYLE   As soon as you're arrested.

DAVID   Are we arrested?

DOYLE   Not yet. (*Pausing a moment*) Would you like a lawyer?

DAVID (*Quickly*)   No, no.

DOYLE (*Indicating the machine*)   I want you to dictate your version of what happened, from the beginning. And anything you say can be used against you.

MIKE (*Uncertain*)   Who first?

DOYLE (*Unsympathetic*)   Either one of you.
   (MIKE *and* DAVID *look at each other.* DAVID *indicates for* MIKE *to start.* MIKE *pulls his chair up to the dictaphone, takes the speaker off the hook, and clears his throat*)

MIKE (*Into speaker*) I was sitting in my office, minding my own business, when the phone rang. "Hello," I said. "Mike, for God's sake, help me," somebody said. "Who is this?" I asked. "It's me, David," he said—

DOYLE (*Annoyed*) Hold it! Hold it! (MIKE *looks at him, inquiringly*) You don't have to start that far back.

MIKE Yes sir.

DOYLE Leave out the dialogue. Just describe why you did it!

MIKE Why I did it?

DOYLE (*Indicating* DAVID) Why you told him to impersonate an F.B.I. agent.

MIKE Yes sir. (*A breath, and into the speaker*) Marriage to me is something sacred. I have never heard the minister intone the sentence, "Whom God hath joined together let un man put asunder," without silently saying "Amen." In my humble opinion the divorce rate in this country is one of the most unfortunate—

DOYLE Hold it! (*He glares at* MIKE) All I want out of you is a simple, clear account of what happened, without a sermon! Or addressing the jury! You'll get that chance!

MIKE Yes sir.
      (*The* SECRETARY *enters*)

SECRETARY Mr. Parker's here. (*She misinterprets* DOYLE's *expression*) He's the man who was here yesterday, from the C.I.A.

DOYLE (*Displeased*) Send him in. Ahh. It had to be him. Sure, he'd know first. It figured. (*The* SECRETARY *exits*) He's come to crow! I tell you if he steps over the line, just one crack too many, I'll hit him with that lamp!

POWELL Take it easy, Bob.

DOYLE He better be careful!
(*The* SECRETARY *admits* PARKER. *He's no friendlier than he was yesterday. He looks hard at* DAVID)

DOYLE (*Testing*) This is Williams. Parker, C.I.A.

DAVID How do you do.

PARKER (*Flat*) How do you do.

DOYLE (*To* PARKER) What is it?

PARKER (*Throwing a tape on the desk*) Another Belka wire tap.

DOYLE (*Just repeating*) Belka.
(DOYLE *puts it on the machine, while* PARKER *looks hard at* DAVID. DAVID *is uncomfortable*)

PARKER Like your picture in the paper, Williams?

DAVID (*Stumped, tries smiling. Hollowly*) Well, it's a good likeness.
(*The machine starts*)

C.I.A. VOICE Telephone conversation of Ladislov Belka intercepted nine-fifteen A.M.
(*Silence, and then the ringing*)

BELKA'S VOICE My name's Harrison. I'm in the Public Relations Department of the F.B.I.

ANN'S VOICE Oh, how do you do.

BELKA'S VOICE (*Jolly*) We've had the hardest job getting through to you.

ANN'S VOICE Well, we had the receiver off the hook because so many strangers were calling up. I hope we didn't inconvenience you.

BELKA'S VOICE That's all right. Would you and your husband come down to room fifteen hundred of the Empire State Building? We'd like to take some photographs of you and your famous husband.

DAVID (*Just recovering*) Say, that's Ann! (DOYLE *flicks the machine, stopping it*) That's my wife! She's not talking to any Belka!

DOYLE Would you mind letting us hear this?

DAVID (*Beginning to comprehend*) He's a—he's a—he's not an F.B.I. man!

DOYLE No, he's not. He's impersonating an F.B.I. man. You've heard of that happening, I imagine.

DAVID Why, he wanted me to . . .
(*He trails off.* DOYLE *flicks the machine on*)

ANN'S VOICE Here's Mr. Williams now. (*Further away, but quite clear*) They want to take my picture too!

DAVID'S VOICE Yes sir?

ANN'S VOICE What shall I wear? My blue. No, my gray!

BELKA'S VOICE (*Hearty*) Harrison here! Don't think we ever met, Williams! Have a teletype on you. Chief wants some photographs of you and the missus! Good publicity for the bureau, you know!

DAVID'S VOICE Yes sir.

ANN'S VOICE No, my blue! Blue photographs better! Thinner!

BELKA'S VOICE Show up at four o'clock in room fifteen hundred of the Empire State Building. It's a cover we use. The door says Atlantic Import and Export Company but you walk right in. Got it? Fifteen hundred, Empire State Building. Be on time now!

DAVID'S VOICE Yes sir.

ANN'S VOICE (*Singing as before*) Tra la la, la—
(*She is abruptly cut off as they hang up*)

DOYLE Right in this building!

POWELL Damn cute!

DOYLE Boy, the juxtaposition's got 'em real bad. They're desperate. (*He looks to* DAVID) They want the names of those doctors.

DAVID From me?

POWELL That'll be a good trick.

106

DAVID They're not going to get anything from me.

MIKE There's a bet I'd like to make. I'd give odds.

PARKER Atlantic Import and Export. That's a new one. We haven't got anything on them.

DOYLE (*To* EVANS) Get the background on that company.

EVANS Right.
(*He exits*)

DOYLE Boy, pull a thread and a whole rug unravels. (*To* PARKER) What do you think they'll try?

PARKER Can't be sure. They want those names. Probably try to trick him into handing them over. They'll try to get the names one way or another.

DOYLE (*Thinking*) Yeah.

DAVID (*A pause*) I could leave town.

PARKER Are you crazy? Do you know what it means to us even to catch them impersonating somebody? We're allowed to take their visas away and throw them out of the country. Those are the rules! Then they have to send new men and it bollixes up their organization for months! We've fallen into something fat!

DOYLE (*Thinking*) Yeah. (*All watch him think. Finally he turns to* PARKER) Parker!

107

PARKER Yeah?

DOYLE You know, rivalry's one thing, coöperation's another! Why don't we make this thing a joint venture?

PARKER (*Indicating* DAVID) You mean including him? The whole thing?

DOYLE Yeah!

PARKER (*Touched*) That's damn generous of you!

DOYLE What the hell!

POWELL Yeah. What the hell! Bunch the whole thing together!
    (PARKER *and* DOYLE *shake on it, fervently*)

PARKER (*To* DAVID) Go get 'em boy! (*A wave*) I got things to do!
    (*And he's out. All look toward* DAVID)

DOYLE Well, maybe you can make up for some of the trouble you caused. You and Mrs. Williams are going to keep that date in room fifteen hundred of the Empire State Building.
    (DOYLE *exits*)

DAVID (*A moment*) I don't want anything to happen to my wife.

POWELL (*He likes* DAVID *for this*) Don't worry. Nothing will happen to her. We'll take every precaution.

DAVID Can't you tell me what's going to happen?

POWELL I'm afraid I can't. Just trust us.

DAVID (*Unhappy*)   Yes sir.
(POWELL *reaches into his pocket, takes out a roll of Tums, and hands them to* DAVID)

The lights dim out

SCENE FOUR

A small cubicle, part of a florist shop, lower left, reveals PARKER *with a portable walkie-talkie.*

PARKER (*Into microphone, low*) Parker calling Doyle, over
  (*Another cubicle of light, upper right, part of room 1502, reveals* DOYLE)

DOYLE (*Into his microphone*) Doyle here, over.

PARKER I've got one man outside, two in the lobby. I'm in the florist shop, clear view of the entrance. Where are you?

DOYLE Room fifteen oh two, across the hall from Atlantic Import and Export. But Belka's not in there. We're sure of that.

PARKER Think he's smelled something?

DOYLE Maybe. Hope not.

PARKER (*Suddenly*) I see him! He's in front of the building! He's waiting! For the Williamses, I guess.

DOYLE Why is he waiting!

PARKER I don't know. He said room fifteen hundred.

DOYLE Something's funny. He ought to be up here.

PARKER Haven't we been able to find anything on Atlantic Import and Export?

DOYLE   Not yet. We're on it. We'll have something in an hour.

PARKER   I can't understand that, neither of us having any background on them. What do they sell?

DOYLE   Rugs and coffee.

PARKER   That's out of Turkey and South America, if they're part of the main apparatus. But they may be a unit by themselves.

DOYLE   I'll bet that's it. They're a cell of their own and this emergency's smoked them out.

PARKER   Yeah. (*Seeing them*) Here come the Williamses! Belka's stopped them. He's introducing himself! He's shaking hands with Mrs. Williams. He's shaking hands with Mr. Williams. Mrs. Williams is kissing Mr. Williams. They're coming into the building! Now they're going through the revolving doors!
   (*Stage center lights up, revealing an elevator with a repair man in it. The control panel has been taken off, and the repair man, in work coveralls, is* ORLOV. *Screwdriver in hand, he sneaks glances to the lobby. A tape, with a sign, "Out of Order," stops people from entering. One person attempts to enter the elevator*)

PARKER   Now they're walking through the lobby!

ORLOV   Out of order! Next car!
   (*The person goes on.* ORLOV *sees someone approaching! He unhooks the blocking tape.* BELKA *appears, escorting* ANN *under the arm;* DAVID *follows.* ANN *hesitates a second on seeing the sign and workman*)

PARKER They're going toward the elevators!

ANN It's out of order!

BELKA Not at all! We ensure secrecy. This is our own elevator.

ANN (*Impressed*) Oh, how exciting! You F.B.I.!
(*They are in,* ORLOV *closes the door*)

PARKER (*Into microphone*) Goddamn it! They went into an
elevator under repair!

DOYLE What?

PARKER There was an out of order elevator with a workman in
it! It must've been a plant, and they're in it!

DOYLE No!

PARKER He never meant to take them to that import office!
And that's why we didn't have anything on them!

DOYLE They're not going to let them out of that elevator!

PARKER I don't think so! We better get them out of there!
(*The elevator doors rise, revealing the elevator interior.
A roller behind the rear wall grill, the sound of air pres-
sure, and some quiver supply the illusion of movement*)

ANN (*Happily excited*) I'm tingly all over!
(ORLOV, *applying his screwdriver to the control panel,
stops the elevator*)

PARKER (*Looking up to where the indicator should be*) Say,
the elevator's stopped!

DOYLE Holy H. mackerel! Where the hell's the master switch-board in this building!
   (*He starts,* PARKER *starts, the lights in their respective cubicles go out*)

ANN Why has the elevator stopped?
   (BELKA *produces a small blue automatic*)

BELKA We will all be very quiet. If possible.

ANN (*The gun is pointing in her direction*) That's a gun!

BELKA That's what it is, madam. And it shoots bullets, not too loudly.

ANN (*Lost*) What's the matter with you?

DAVID They're not F.B.I. men!

ANN They're not?

BELKA No, madam, we are not.
   (ORLOV *has come behind* ANN, *in readiness*)

ANN Who are you?

BELKA I'm sure your husband can tell you.
   (ANN *looks to* DAVID)

DAVID They're foreign agents, Ann!
   (ANN *looks from him to* BELKA *and the gun, and then opens her mouth preparatory to screaming.* ORLOV *has anticipated this and clasps his arm around her throat, from behind. Since her windpipe is obstructed, only a gargled screech comes out. She faints*)

ORLOV Quiet! Quiet!
(*The sight of* ANN *going limp galvanizes* DAVID *into action. He leaps at* ORLOV, *turning his back on* BELKA)

DAVID Get your hands off her—
(BELKA *expertly clips* DAVID *on the back of the neck with the butt of the gun.* DAVID *slumps,* BELKA *seats him on the stool. Both men look at him, unperturbed, since this has evidently been anticipated.* ORLOV *has pressed a small cotton wad over* ANN's *nose, letting her slide to the floor, against the back wall, in a sitting position*)

BELKA That was an amateur move. For an F.B.I. man he isn't very well trained.

ORLOV Fear for his wife overcame his training. We may take advantage of that.
(BELKA *throws him an admiring glance*)

BELKA It's possible you do know your job.

ORLOV I know my job (*Indicating the cotton pad he is now discarding*) Chloroform. (*He takes a kit from his pocket, extracting a hypodermic needle. He prepares to inject* DAVID) This is mainly sodium pentothal, with approximately ten minutes' effectiveness. During that time he should reveal what he knows. (*He injects* DAVID) His will to resist is now lessened. How much lessened is a matter of his character. If he is strong-minded, and loyal, it is slightly more difficult.

BELKA (*Looking at* DAVID *intently*) He may be loyal, but he doesn't look strong-minded.

ORLOV One never can tell.

114

BELKA Well, go on! Begin!
(ORLOV *lifts* DAVID'S *head.* DAVID *has a far-off, relaxed expression.* ORLOV *leans close to him*)

ORLOV (*Friendly voice*) Hello.

DAVID (*Calm*) Hello.

ORLOV What's your name, my friend?

DAVID David Williams. What's your name?

ORLOV You don't care about my name. And what do you do, David?

DAVID I'm assistant professor of Chemistry at Columbia University.

ORLOV And what else do you do? (*No answer*) There must be something else you do?

DAVID I'm in charge of admissions.

ORLOV (*Encouraged*) Yes. And what else, David? (*No answer*) What else do you do with your time? At night, for instance?

DAVID I go bowling.

ORLOV (*To* BELKA) It's a sport.

BELKA I know what bowling is!

ORLOV He's blocking out his F.B.I. identity. He may have more character than he looks.

BELKA Ask him the names of the doctors and scientists.

ORLOV It's not wise to ask direct questions (*Charm voice again*) Let's play a little game, David. Do you like doctors? (*No answer*) Are there any doctors you dislike?

DAVID (*Slowly*) Dr. . . . Eberstad.
(ORLOV *and* BELKA *exchange a quick glance*)

ORLOV Eberstad?

BELKA I think there's an Eberstad in radioactivity! (*Eagerly, to* DAVID) What is Dr. Eberstad doing?

ORLOV No direct questions!

DAVID He's making a bridge.

BELKA A bridge! (*A deprecating glance to* ORLOV) Where is the bridge? Where will it be?

DAVID On my upper left molar.

ORLOV (*He gives* BELKA *a belittling look*) May I? I'm going to induce fear. (*Harsh tone*) David Williams!

DAVID Yes?

ORLOV Do you love your wife?

DAVID Yes, I do.

ORLOV You wouldn't want anything to happen to her?

DAVID No, I wouldn't.

ORLOV (*Closer to him*) If you don't want any harm to befall her—terrible harm—tell me the names of the men working on the secret projects! (DAVID *doesn't answer*) You're never going to see your wife again!

DAVID (*The most animation he's shown*)   Don't leave me, Ann! Don't!
(BELKA *shakes* ORLOV's *shoulder*)

BELKA   You've hit on something!

ORLOV (*Pursuing it*)   No, you're not going to see her any more!

DAVID   But I love her.

ORLOV (*As though talking to a child*)   We're going to take you in a boat far out to sea, and then we'll transfer you to a submarine, and then this submarine will go deep down where nobody can find it, and it'll take you away.

DAVID   A submarine?

ORLOV   A big submarine. And you'll never see your wife any more.

DAVID   Never?

ORLOV   Never! (*David begins to cry*) Sentimental! He's a difficult subject. So many different facets!
(*They watch him, stumped. The lower right section of the stage lights up, revealing* DOYLE *and* PARKER *at a switchboard which has been opened, showing a panel of different colored wires*)

DOYLE (*Fingering the wire*)   The contact's broken in the elevator!

PARKER   Try to short it! Maybe that'll release it!
(*There is buzzing from the elevator panel, which is the result of* DOYLE's *action.* ORLOV *and* BELKA *look up, trying to locate the sound*)

117

BELKA They're doing something! What do you think they know?

ORLOV That the elevator's out of order. That's all. (*Thinking*) What's bad is they may immobilize the circuit. Then *we* can't move it. (*Another pause*) I suggest we take the elevator to the basement.

BELKA Why the basement? Won't there be people there?

ORLOV There are three basements. The bottom level is just machinery.
    (*He steps to the panel, applies his screwdriver, and the elevator starts to descend, the roller effect behind the grill going in reverse, as the lights dim*)

DOYLE (*Jumping*) Damn!

PARKER What's the matter?

DOYLE I got a shock.

PARKER Maybe the circuit's on?

DOYLE (*Pointing*) Wouldn't the elevator be moving? It'd show on here, wouldn't it?

PARKER (*Looking*) Yeah. It's not moving.
    (*We still see the elevator moving, and then it blacks out*)

DOYLE What the hell do we do now?

PARKER I wonder what they're doing to him to get those names.

DOYLE (*Grim thoughts*) Never mind the names. What are they doing to his wife?

118

PARKER (*Bitterly*) We're awful bright! Atlantic Export and Import Company!

DOYLE (*He puts his transmitter on*) Evans!
(*The lower left part of the stage lights up, showing* EVANS *and his transmitter*)

EVANS Evans here!

DOYLE The elevator won't move! Give me the disposition of your men.

EVANS We've blocked off every street exit, both stairways, and there are two men on the roof. They may get off at one of the floors, we haven't enough men to cover them all, but they'll never get out of the building!
(*This light dims out as the boiler room lights up. Through the metal door, down three metal steps, come* BELKA, ORLOV, DAVID, *and* ANN. *They close the door behind them.* BELKA, *carrying* ANN, *deposits her on a drum in the corner.* ORLOV *supports* DAVID. *Have you ever seen a boiler room? It throbs and whines. Indicators move on gauges, and the very floor throbs with pulsing power. To come to the point, you can't tell a boiler room from the inside of a submarine*)

ORLOV This is the boiler room. Nobody comes here!
(ORLOV *props* DAVID *between two vertical pipes, his arms over the valves.* DAVID *is conscious but without a will of his own*)

DAVID (*Tearful*) I'm sorry about what happened, Ann. It'll never happen again.

BELKA What is he talking about?

ORLOV His wife! He won't leave the subject. (*He looks at his watch*) And we haven't so much time before the pentothal wears off.

BELKA Can't you give him another dose?

ORLOV (*He shakes his head*) Put him to sleep. (*He snaps his fingers at* DAVID) Come on now, Williams! Forget your wife! Forget her!

DAVID I'll never forget her! As long as I live!

ORLOV He's obsessed with the subject!

BELKA (*Grabbing him by the collar*) Forget her, do you hear! Put her out of your mind!

DAVID (*Vehemently*) Never! I love her! And she loves me!

ORLOV (*Ingratiating again*) David?

DAVID Yes.

ORLOV You'd do anything your wife asked you to, wouldn't you?

DAVID Anything.

ORLOV She wants you to give us the names of the people working on the secret projects.
(DAVID *smiles;* BELKA *and* ORLOV *hold their breaths*)

BELKA (*Soft*) Good! Good!

DAVID (*Slowly*) But I can't do that.

BELKA (*Impatient—loud*) Why can't you? Why not?

DAVID (*He laughs*)   I can't. Not if you tortured me. With red-hot coals.

ORLOV (*To* BELKA)   He's remarkable. I've never seen a man conquer his subconscious so completely.

BELKA   I'm not interested in admiring him!
(*Stumped, they both look at* DAVID. DAVID *smiles at them and crooks his finger, indicating to* BELKA *to come closer*)

DAVID   Come here. I want to whisper something to you.

ORLOV   Go on!
(BELKA *comes closer, hopefully. He is real close to* DAVID. DAVID *kisses him,* BELKA *jumps back a foot and curses in Russian*)

DAVID   You're a pretty girl, Ann.

ORLOV (*Scientific*)   He thinks you're his wife.

BELKA   Well, he's wrong!

ORLOV   Maybe if you'd let him kiss you a little—

BELKA   You kiss him!

ORLOV   He likes you.

BELKA   I'm the superior here! You kiss him! That's an order!
(ANN *stirs noisily, attracting their attention*)

ORLOV (*Merely a comment, not concerned about her*)   She's waking up.

BELKA (*A cursory glance at* ANN, *then back to his absorption with* DAVID)   Can we do anything else to him?

ORLOV   No. And the pentothal's wearing off!

BELKA   (*He considers a moment. Disgustedly*)   Aaah!

ORLOV   They'll investigate the elevator. I suggest we leave here. (BELKA *looks hard at* DAVID, *reluctant to go, finally decides to, swears in Russian, and starts out, followed by* ORLOV. *The door closes behind them.* ANN *comes to. She crosses woozily, passing* DAVID. *Then sees him and walks over to him*)

ANN   (*Alarmed*)   David! David! (*He smiles sleepily*) Speak to me!

DAVID   How do you do, ma'am.

ANN   Are you all right? (*She waves her hand before his eyes*) What's the matter with you? David! They gave you something! (DAVID *merely smiles broader*) My darling! (*It occurs to her*) David, did you tell them the names of the secret scientists at Columbia University?

DAVID   No.

ANN   Oh, I'm proud of you, David. Pull yourself together.

DAVID   You pull yourself together! I'm going to jail for a hundred and eighty years! (*A plea*) Wait for me.

ANN   (*Slightly aware of something*)   Why would you be going to jail?

DAVID   Because it's against the law to print fake F.B.I. cards.

ANN   (*Slowly*)   Fake F.B.I. cards? Where did you get that F.B.I. card?

DAVID Mike had it printed at CBS. We got the gun there too. It's very interesting over there. You ought to go sometime.

ANN (*Still not sure*) You're not an F.B.I. man?

DAVID Me, in the F.B.I.? Why, I couldn't even get to be an Eagle Scout, you jackass!

ANN (*She is trying to think back, fitting all the pieces together*) Is Mr. Powell an F.B.I. man?

DAVID Oh yes, he's a real agent. Only Mike and I are fakes.

ANN What about those two women you took to Lee Wong's restaurant?

DAVID Oh, they're real women.

ANN What do they do?

DAVID They sing and dance like rabbits.

ANN Why, you—
(*She turns in wild frustration, looking for something with which to hit him, and spies a firepail of water. She throws it in his face. She stamps in rage, turns, and strides to the door. She opens it, hurries out, and slams it shut after her. DAVID is coming out of his sleep. The switchboard inset lights up, revealing PARKER and DOYLE still tinkering with it. DOYLE is working with the screwdriver; PARKER is watching*)

PARKER Try that circuit on the left! (DOYLE *does. There is a small flash from the switchboard, and a large flash in the boiler room. The main lights go out, leaving two red emer-*

123

gency lamps aglow. DAVID *is not yet conscious*) What did that
do?

> (*The switchboard inset blacks out.* DAVID *is now con-
> scious. He looks around*)

DAVID   My God, I'm in a submarine!
> (*He moves around unsteadily; he walks toward the
> door. He tries it and discovers that it's locked. He starts to
> cry. He walks slowly, sniffling, looking around, reach-
> ing the drum. He sits on it, cries audibly again. A valve
> hisses near him. He jumps. He cries again. His jumping
> has thrown his weight against a handle, and a rotor be-
> gins to whirl. He takes the handle, idly. He moves it,
> and the revolving disc goes faster, the noise altering. He
> looks at it. He moves the handle back, the wheel slows
> down, the noise reverts. He tries it again, moves it back
> once more. Then, in the midst of his sniffling, an idea
> occurs to him. He looks with dread toward the door*)

DAVID   I'll sink it!
> (*He goes to the door and locks it from the inside. Now,
> reluctantly, he goes about scuttling the submarine, con-
> tinually sniffling and crying. Each turn of the valve
> wheel is an effort of an unheroic will. The first wheel
> causes a huge gurgling. The second whines. Two levers
> cause flash explosions. The last wheel produces a dive-
> bombing effect, culminating in an explosion and a pipe
> breaking loose. Smoke begins to pour from its dangling
> end. The pressure has cracked the pipes above him and
> water begins to stream down. He now stands between
> the two upright pipes, grasping each one, the water pour-
> ing on him. He begins to sing "America, the Beautiful."
> As he begins the second chorus, the insets come on*)

FIRST EMPIRE STATE TENANT Hello, superintendent? What's happened? We're broiling! The temperature is over a hundred!
(*Light out. A second inset lights up. Unidentifiable man at phone, coat collar up*)

SECOND EMPIRE STATE TENANT Cut that air conditioning! We're freezing! Our office is below zero!
(*Light out. Third inset lights up. Unidentifiable man, into phone*)

EMPIRE STATE BUILDING EMPLOYEE McCarthy! (*Shouting*) The even number floors are boiling, the odd numbers are freezing!
(*Light out. Fourth inset. Unidentifiable woman, on phone*)

THIRD EMPIRE STATE TENANT (*A screech*) Steam is coming out of the top floor! The wallpaper's peeling off!
(*Light out. We come back to* DAVID, *still singing. There is pounding at the door. He stops singing, walks toward the door, and shakes his fist at it*)

DAVID How do you like it? Die like rats in a trap! You swine! You murderers!

(*He goes back to his position at the pipes and resumes singing. The door breaks through, admitting* MCCARTHY, POWELL *and* PARKER. DAVID *looks at them in amazement,* "America, the Beautiful" *trailing off.* MCCARTHY *turns off the water and noise.* POWELL *turns on the original lighing*)

POWELL (*Pulling* DAVID *out from behind pipe*) Get out of that!

DAVID Where are we? Aren't we in a submarine?

POWELL You're in the basement of the Empire State Building and you've damned near ruined it!

DAVID We are?

MIKE (*Appearing in the doorway*) Hey, everybody! (*They all turn toward him*) Come and see where Doyle caught the spies! They're swimming around in the bottom of the elevator shaft! Like two goddamned goldfish!
(POWELL, PARKER *and* MCCARTHY *rush by* MIKE, *and out of the room*)

DAVID (*Looks at* MIKE, *fearful*) Where's Ann?

MIKE (*Nods*) They gave you something. You talked. She knows everything.

DAVID Oh.

MIKE Well, they didn't get the names of those secret scientists out of you. You can feel happy about that.

DAVID (*Sitting on the step of the doorway*) I'll never be happy again.

MIKE Now, now.

DAVID (*Shakes his head sadly*) Ann hates me.

MIKE Oh, I don't know. When she heard you were down here turning on all the steam taps, she got real excited. Doyle thought you might be scalded alive. She screamed pretty loud.

DAVID (*Hopefully*) She did?

126

MIKE (*He nods*)   Got real hysterical for a while.

DAVID (*Thinks about it and deflates again*)   She's got a soft heart. But she's not forgiving. (MIKE *crosses behind him, standing in the doorway*) That's not one of her qualities.
(MIKE *reaches into the doorway and gently leads the waiting* ANN *out*)

MIKE (*Leading* DAVID *on*)   But she has got other qualities?

DAVID   Oh, she has. She has.

MIKE   Has she really? I never noticed.

DAVID   Oh yes.

MIKE   What, for instance?
(ANN *looks down at* DAVID *with great tenderness.* MIKE *looks at them, turns off the light, which leaves a red glow, and withdraws. To* DAVID, *the change of light is normal*)

DAVID   She's got one great quality, Mike. (*Music starts sneaking in*) Every girl should have it. I know that now. She's insanely jealous. That's a wonderful quality in a woman. I wouldn't want a girl who wasn't jealous. If she's extra jealous, what does that prove? Only that she's extra in love. (ANN *can hardly refrain from putting loving hands on him. She starts, but holds back*) I sure wish I had my girl back again. I wouldn't let an exchange student kiss me if her life depended on it! I'd wear blinders! I'd grow a beard! I'd—(ANN *puts her hand over his mouth. It's obviously a woman's hand, not* MIKE'S. *He turns slowly and looks at her. Lost in the wonder of it, he doesn't move*) Ann!

127

WHO WAS THAT LADY I SAW YOU WITH?

ANN Come on home, my darling!
      (*He gets up, they look at each other a long moment,
      they embrace and kiss*)

      The curtain falls

128